Recipes

American Cooking: Creole and Acadian

Contents

Foods of the World

TIME-LIFE BOOKS, NEW YORK

Introductory Notes

Scallions and Shallots: A Question of Names

The common names of vegetables do not always follow strict botanical terminology. Fresh chicory leaves, for example, are called curly endive, although the two plants are only cousins, and broad-leaved endive is known as escarole. But few kitchen plants can match the terminological confusion over the common scallion—especially in Louisiana.

The vegetable that most cooks call a scallion may be any of three different kinds of onion: a green onion, a bunching onion or a green shallot. *Green onions* are the shoots of any white onion, harvested before the onion bulb has formed. They grow as individual plants and would, if left in the field to mature and dry, develop large white or yellow globes. (Though they are now harvested year round, they are still sometimes called "spring" onions). *Bunching onions* grow in clusters on enlarged root bases. They do not develop into globes and are eaten only as scallions. *Shallots* are still another member of the onion family. Like bunching onions, they grow in clusters, with anywhere from 5 to 40 bulbs on a single root. Each bulb sends up a shoot and, when the young bulbs are separated for marketing, they have the same white elongated bases and green tops that scallions do, and a similarly pungent flavor. When shallots are left in the ground to mature and dry, the bulbs swell and separate somewhat. At this stage, they look like large colorful garlic cloves, but their flavor is far milder than that of garlic.

In Louisiana, which produces about 90 per cent of the shallots grown in the United States, the shallot crop is sold and used in its green form. For this reason, perhaps, a special problem of terminology has developed there. Since the green shallot is the most readily available form of scallion in Louisiana, the term scallion is usually restricted to that vegetable in Creole and Acadian cooking. Elsewhere in the United States, the term scallion usually refers to a green or bunching onion, while a shallot is the mature vegetable, usually reddish brown, clove-shaped and dried. (Most of these mature shallots are grown in New Jersey and New York or imported from France or Mexico.)

Fortunately, the average cook need not concern herself with this bewildering cluster of names. In their green forms, onions and shallots taste much alike and play identical roles in cooking; in this book, the term scallion is correctly used to refer to the green forms of these vegetables, and a cook can use whatever is sold under that name at her grocer's.

Brown Roux

To make about 11 tablespoons

8 tablespoons unsifted all-purpose
    flour
8 tablespoons vegetable oil

Although the term roux is familiar in French cooking, the kind of brown roux used in Louisiana is unique. Flour and fat (usually vegetable oil) are cooked slowly until the mixture is brown and has a nutlike aroma and taste. This brown roux then serves as the base and thickening agent for bisques, gumbos and other soups, as well as for gravies and stews.

Combine the flour and oil in a heavy 10-inch skillet (preferably cast-iron or enameled iron) and, with a large metal spatula, stir them to a smooth paste. Place the skillet over the lowest possible heat and, stirring constantly, simmer the *roux* slowly for 45 minutes to an hour.

After 5 minutes or so the mixture will begin to foam and this foaming may continue for as long as 10 minutes. After about half an hour, the *roux* will begin to darken and have a faintly nutty aroma. Continue to cook slowly, stirring with the spatula, until the *roux* is a dark rich brown. (During the last 5 minutes or so of cooking, the *roux* darkens quickly and you may want to lift the pan from the heat periodically to let it cool. Should the *roux* burn, discard it and make another batch.)

Immediately scrape the contents of the skillet into a small bowl. Let the *roux* cool to room temperature, then cover with foil or plastic wrap and refrigerate it until ready to use. (It can safely be kept for weeks.)

When it cools the *roux* will separate and the fat will rise to the surface. Before using the *roux,* stir it briefly to recombine it. Measure the desired amount into the pan and warm the *roux* slowly over low heat, stirring constantly. Whether added immediately or not, any liquid that is to be incorporated with the brown *roux* must be at least lukewarm or the mixture may separate. If it does, beat it together again with a whisk.

Techniques for Home Canning

To ensure consistent results in home canning, use standard canning jars or jelly glasses with matching lids. Examine each jar or glass carefully and discard those with loose covers and those with cracked or chipped edges. An airtight seal is essential to prevent food spoilage.

Wash the jars, glasses, lids and rubber rings in hot soapy water and rinse them in scalding water. Place them in a large deep pot and pour in enough hot water to cover them completely. Bring to a boil over high heat, then turn off the heat while you finish cooking the food that you plan to can. The jars or glasses must be hot when they are filled. (If you have a dishwasher with a sanitizing cycle, simply run the jars, glasses, lids and rings through the cycle, using your usual dishwashing powder, and leave them in the closed machine until you are ready to can.)

To prepare for sealing the glasses, grate a 4-ounce bar of paraffin into the top of a double boiler (preferably one with a pouring spout), and melt the paraffin over hot water.

When the food is ready for canning, lift the jars or glasses from the pot or dishwasher with tongs and stand them upright on a level surface. Leave the lids and rings in the pot (or dishwasher) until you are ready to use them. Fill and seal the jars one at a time, filling each jar to within ⅛ inch of the top or each glass to within ½ inch of the top. Each jar should be sealed quickly and tightly with its ring and lid. (If there is not enough food to fill the last jar or glass completely, do not attempt to seal it. Refrigerate and use within the next week.)

The jelly glasses also should be sealed at once. Pour a single thin layer of hot paraffin over the surface of the jelly, making sure it covers the jelly completely and touches the glass on all sides. If air bubbles appear on the paraffin, prick them immediately with the tip of a knife. Let the glasses rest until the paraffin cools and hardens, then cover with metal lids.

If a recipe calls for finishing the preserving process with a water bath, place the filled and sealed jars side by side on a rack in a canner or other deep large pot. Pour in enough hot (not boiling) water to cover the jars by at least 1 inch, securely cover the pot with its lid, and bring to a boil over moderate heat. Boil for the time recommended in the particular recipe. Then, with tongs, remove the jars from the pot and let them cool at room temperature for about 12 hours. Test the seal by pressing the center of each lid with your forefinger. If the inner lid remains in place, unscrew the outer ring, leaving the seal intact. Store the jar upright in a cool, dry, dark spot. If the lid moves at all, the jar is not properly sealed; in that event, refrigerate and serve the food within a week.

4

For additional information on canning, see "How to Make Jellies, Jams and Preserves at Home," USDA Home and Garden Bulletin No. 56, and "Making Pickles and Relishes at Home," USDA Home and Garden Bulletin No. 92. These bulletins cost 15 cents each and can be ordered from the Superintendent of Documents, U.S. Government Printing Office, Washington, D.C. 20402.

Hollandaise Sauce

To make about 1½ cups

½ pound plus 4 tablespoons unsalted butter, cut into ½-inch bits
4 egg yolks

1 tablespoon cold water
2 tablespoons strained fresh lemon juice
¼ teaspoon ground white pepper
½ teaspoon salt

In a small heavy skillet, melt the butter bits over moderate heat, stirring so that they melt completely without browning. Remove the skillet from the heat and cover tightly to keep the melted butter warm.

Combine the egg yolks and water in a 1½- to 2-quart enameled or stainless-steel saucepan and beat vigorously with a wire whisk until the mixture is foamy. Place the pan over the lowest possible heat and continue whisking until the mixture thickens and almost doubles in volume. Do not let the yolks come anywhere near a boil or they will curdle; if necessary, lift the pan off the heat from time to time to cool it.

Still whisking constantly, pour in the reserved hot butter as slowly as possible, and continue to beat over low heat until the sauce thickens heavily. Beat in the lemon juice, pepper and salt, and taste the hollandaise sauce for seasoning.

Serve at once or, if you like, set the pan in a bowl of hot water and keep the sauce warm for up to 30 minutes before serving.

Fish Stock

To make about 1 quart

1½ pounds fish trimmings: the heads, tails and bones of any firm white fish
1 quart cold water
½ cup coarsely chopped onions
¼ cup coarsely chopped celery, including the leaves
1 small bay leaf
¼ teaspoon crumbled dried thyme
½ teaspoon salt
3 whole black peppercorns

Wash the fish trimmings in a deep bowl set under cold running water. Drain, then mash the pieces of fish with the back of a large spoon.

Place the mashed fish in a 3- to 4-quart enameled or stainless-steel saucepan and pour in the water. Bring slowly to a simmer over moderate heat and cook uncovered for 5 minutes, skimming off the foam and scum as they rise to the surface. Add the onions, celery, bay leaf, thyme, salt and peppercorns, and reduce the heat to low. Simmer partially covered for 30 minutes, skimming the surface from time to time.

Remove the pan from the heat and, with a slotted spoon, lift out and discard the fish and vegetables. Strain the stock into a deep bowl through a fine sieve lined with a double thickness of dampened cheesecloth. The stock will keep refrigerated for 2 or 3 days or it can be cooled to room temperature, covered tightly and frozen.

How to Handle Hot Chilies

Hot chilies are cousins to the familiar green bell peppers, but they require special handling. Their volatile oils may make your skin tingle and your eyes burn. While working with the chilies, wear rubber gloves if you can and be careful not to touch your face. To prepare chilies, rinse them clean under cold running water. (Hot water may cause fumes to rise from dried chilies, and even these fumes can irritate your nose and eyes.) Cut or break off the stems if you wish to leave the seeds (the hottest parts of chilies) in the pods. If a chili is to be seeded, pull out the stem and the seeds with your gloved fingers. In most cases the ribs inside are thin, but if they seem thick and fleshy you may cut them out with a small sharp knife. Follow the instructions in the recipes for slicing or chopping chilies. After handling hot chilies it is essential that you wash your hands and gloves thoroughly with soap and water.

APPETIZERS

Deep-fried Catfish Appetizers

To make 8 dozen

1 pound catfish fillets, skinned and cut into 1-inch pieces
1 teaspoon ground hot red pepper (cayenne)
4 teaspoons salt

4 eggs, lightly beaten
2 cups corn flour *(see Glossary, page 150)*, or substitute 2 cups all-purpose flour
Vegetable oil for deep frying
Creole tartar sauce *(page 60)*

Pat the pieces of catfish completely dry with paper towels and season them on all sides with the red pepper and salt. Immerse the pieces, three or four at a time, in the beaten eggs, then roll them about in the flour to coat them evenly. As you proceed, arrange the coated pieces of catfish in one layer on wax paper.

Preheat the oven to its lowest setting. At the same time, line a large shallow baking dish with a double thickness of paper towels and place it in the middle of the oven.

Pour vegetable oil into a deep fryer or large heavy saucepan to a depth of 2 or 3 inches and heat the oil until it reaches a temperature of 375° on a deep-frying thermometer.

Deep-fry the catfish, seven or eight pieces at a time, turning them about with a slotted spoon for about 3 minutes, or until they are crisp and golden brown. As they brown, transfer the finished pieces to the paper-lined dish and keep them warm in the oven while you deep-fry the rest.

To serve, arrange the catfish attractively on a large heated platter and insert a toothpick into each piece. Spoon the Creole tartar sauce into a bowl and present it separately.

Crabmeat Crêpes

To serve 4 as a main dish or 8 as a
   first course

CRÊPES
½ cup unsifted flour
⅛ teaspoon salt
2 eggs

½ cup milk
2 to 4 tablespoons melted butter

1 tablespoon butter, softened

To prepare the crêpes, combine the ½ cup of flour and ⅛ teaspoon of salt and sift them into a deep bowl. Add the eggs and stir with a wire whisk until the batter is smooth. Whisking constantly, pour in the milk in a slow, thin stream. Cover the bowl tightly with plastic wrap and let the batter rest at room temperature for about 1 hour before using it.

Heat an 8-inch crêpe pan or skillet over high heat until a drop of water flicked into it evaporates instantly. With a pastry brush, lightly grease the bottom and sides of the pan with a little of the melted butter. Pour about ¼ cup of the batter into the pan and tip the pan so that the batter quickly covers the bottom; the batter should cling to the pan and begin to firm up almost immediately.

At once tilt the pan over the bowl and pour off any excess batter; the finished crêpe should be paper thin. Cook the crêpe for a minute or so, until a rim of brown shows around the edge. Turn it over with a spatula and cook the other side for a minute longer. Slide the crêpe onto a plate. Then brush melted butter on the skillet again and proceed with the rest of the crêpes; you should have enough ingredients to make eight or nine in all. The crêpes may be made hours or even days ahead of time and kept, tightly covered, in the refrigerator or freezer. If you do this, let them return to room temperature before attempting to separate them.

Preheat the oven to 400°. With a pastry brush, spread the tablespoon of softened butter evenly over the bottom and sides of a 13-by-9-by-2-inch baking-serving dish, and set it aside.

SAUCE AND FILLING
4 tablespoons butter, cut into small
   bits
½ cup finely chopped scallions
¼ cup flour
1½ cups chicken stock, fresh or
   canned
½ cup dry white wine
¼ teaspoon ground hot red pepper
   (cayenne)

½ teaspoon salt
2 egg yolks, lightly beaten
1½ cups fresh, frozen or canned
   crabmeat, thoroughly drained and
   picked over to remove all bits of
   shell and cartilage
2 tablespoons finely chopped fresh
   parsley, preferably the flat-leaf
   Italian variety

To prepare the sauce and filling, melt the 4 tablespoons of butter bits over moderate heat in a heavy 1- to 1½-quart saucepan. When the foam begins to subside, add the scallions and, stirring frequently, cook for about 5 minutes, or until they are soft but not brown. Add the ¼ cup of flour and mix well. Stirring constantly with a wire whisk, pour in the chicken stock and wine in a slow, thin stream and cook over high heat until the sauce mixture comes to a boil, thickens lightly and is smooth.

Stir in the red pepper and the ½ teaspoon of salt, reduce the heat to low and simmer for about 3 minutes to remove any taste of raw flour. Ladle about 3 tablespoons of the sauce into the beaten egg yolks and whisk together thoroughly. Then, whisking the mixture constantly, pour the egg yolks slowly into the sauce and simmer for 2 or 3 minutes longer to cook the egg yolks. Do not let the sauce come anywhere near a boil or the yolks will curdle. Taste for seasoning.

Ladle 1 cup of the sauce into a bowl and stir in the crabmeat. Set the remaining sauce aside off the heat.

Place 3 tablespoons of the crabmeat mixture on the lower third of each crêpe and roll it up into a cylinder; do not tuck in the ends. Arrange the filled crêpes side by side in the buttered baking dish and pour the reserved sauce over the center of the row of crêpes, leaving the ends unsauced. Bake in the upper third of the oven for 10 minutes, or until the sauce bubbles. Sprinkle the crêpes with the parsley and serve at once, directly from the baking dish.

Stuffed Crabs

To serve 6 as a first course

1 tablespoon butter, softened, plus 7 tablespoons butter, cut into ½-inch bits
2 cups plus 2 tablespoons soft fresh crumbs made from French- or Italian-type white bread, pulverized in a blender
¼ cup fish stock *(page 6)* or ¼ cup fresh or bottled clam broth
¼ cup finely chopped onions
¾ pound fresh, frozen or canned crabmeat, thoroughly drained and picked over to remove all bits of shell and cartilage
½ cup finely chopped scallions, including 3 inches of the green tops
2 tablespoons finely chopped fresh parsley, preferably the flat-leaf Italian variety
½ teaspoon ground hot red pepper (cayenne)
½ teaspoon salt

Preheat the oven to 400°. With a pastry brush, spread the tablespoon of softened butter evenly over the bottoms of six medium-sized natural or ceramic crab or scallop shells. Combine 2 cups of the bread crumbs with the fish stock or clam broth in a bowl, mix well and set aside.

In a heavy 10-inch skillet, melt 4 tablespoons of the butter bits over moderate heat. Add the onions and, stirring frequently, cook for about 5

Continued on next page

minutes, or until they are soft and translucent but not brown. Remove the skillet from the heat and stir in the moistened bread crumbs, the crabmeat, scallions, parsley, red pepper and salt. Taste for seasoning.

Spoon the crabmeat mixture into the buttered shells, dividing it equally among them and slightly mounding the centers. Sprinkle the remaining 2 tablespoons of bread crumbs and the remaining 3 tablespoons of butter bits over the tops and arrange the crab or scallop shells side by side in a large shallow baking dish.

Bake the stuffed crabs in the upper third of the oven for 15 minutes, then slide them under the broiler for 30 seconds or so to brown the tops, if desired. Serve at once, directly from the shells.

Shrimp Remoulade

To serve 6 to 8 as a first course

¼ cup Creole mustard (see
    Glossary, page 150)
2 tablespoons paprika
1 teaspoon ground hot red pepper
    (cayenne)
5 teaspoons salt
½ cup tarragon vinegar
1⅓ cups olive oil
1½ cups coarsely chopped
    scallions, including 3 inches of

the green tops
½ cup very finely chopped celery
½ cup coarsely chopped fresh
    parsley, preferably the flat-leaf
    Italian variety
3 pounds medium-sized uncooked
    shrimp (about 20 to 24 to a
    pound)
1 large iceberg lettuce, trimmed,
    quartered lengthwise and cut into
    ¼-inch-wide shreds

To prepare the remoulade sauce, combine the mustard, paprika, red pepper and 4 teaspoons of the salt in a deep bowl and stir with a wire whisk until all the ingredients are thoroughly combined. Beat in the vinegar. Then, whisking constantly, pour in the oil in a slow, thin stream and continue to beat until the sauce is smooth and thick. Add the scallions, celery and parsley, and mix well. Cover the bowl tightly with plastic wrap and let the sauce rest at room temperature for at least 4 hours before serving.

Meanwhile, shell the shrimp. Devein them by making a shallow incision down their backs with a small sharp knife and lifting out the black or white intestinal vein with the point of the knife. Wash the shrimp briefly in a sieve or colander set under cold running water.

Bring 2 quarts of water and the remaining teaspoon of salt to a simmer over moderate heat, drop in the shrimp and cook uncovered for 3 to 5 minutes, until the shrimp are pink and firm. With a slotted spoon, transfer the shrimp to a plate to cool. Then chill them until ready to serve.

Just before serving, mound the shredded lettuce attractively on six to eight chilled individual serving plates and arrange the shrimp on top. Spoon the remoulade sauce over the shrimp and serve at once.

Headcheese

To make one 9-by-9-by-2-inch loaf

4½ pounds fresh pigs' feet
2 pounds fresh pig's heart, trimmed of excess fat and thoroughly washed
1 pound fresh pig's tongue, trimmed of excess fat
4 quarts water
¼ cup plus 2 teaspoons salt
1 tablespoon cider vinegar
4 tablespoons (¼ cup) strained fresh lemon juice
2 tablespoons butter
1 cup finely chopped onions

1 medium-sized bay leaf, finely crumbled
1 teaspoon ground sage
¼ teaspoon ground mace
½ teaspoon ground hot red pepper (cayenne)
1 teaspoon freshly ground black pepper
1 cup finely chopped fresh parsley, preferably the flat-leaf Italian variety
1 cup finely chopped scallions, including 3 inches of the green tops

On the farms of South Louisiana, this savory jellied meat is made from the head of a hog. The following recipe uses instead fresh pigs' feet, tongue and heart, because these ingredients are more readily available from most retail butchers.

Place the pig's feet, heart and tongue in an 8- to 10-quart enameled or stainless-steel pot and add the water, ¼ cup of the salt, the vinegar and 1 tablespoon of the lemon juice. Bring to a boil over high heat, meanwhile skimming off the foam and scum as they rise to the surface. Then reduce the heat to low, cover partially, and simmer for about 4 hours, or until all the meats are tender and show no resistance when pierced deeply with the point of a sharp knife.

With tongs, transfer the tongue, feet and heart to a cutting board. Measure and reserve 3½ cups of the cooking liquid. While it is still warm, skin the tongue with a small sharp knife, cutting away the fat, bones and gristle at its base. Cut or pull off the meat from the pigs' feet and discard the bones, skin, gristle and fat. Slice the pig's heart lengthwise into quarters and cut away the arteries and veins and any pieces of fat. Cut all the meats into small chunks and put them through the coarsest blade of a food grinder. There should be about 5½ cups of ground meat.

In a heavy 12-inch skillet, melt the butter over moderate heat. Add the onions and, stirring frequently, cook for about 5 minutes, or until they are soft and translucent but not brown.

Pour in ½ cup of the reserved cooking liquid and, stirring from time to time, simmer over low heat for 15 to 20 minutes, until almost all of the liquid has evaporated.

Continued on next page

Stir in the ground meat, the remaining 3 cups of cooking liquid, 3 tablespoons of lemon juice and 2 teaspoons of salt. Add the bay leaf, sage, mace and red and black pepper, and bring to a boil over high heat. Reduce the heat to low and simmer, partially covered, for 10 minutes longer.

Remove the skillet from the heat, stir in the parsley and scallions, and taste for seasoning. With a rubber spatula, transfer the entire contents of the skillet to a 9-by-9-by-2-inch baking dish and smooth the top with the spatula. Cool to room temperature, then cover with foil or plastic wrap and refrigerate for at least 4 hours, or until the headcheese is thoroughly chilled and firm to the touch.

To unmold and serve the headcheese, run a thin-bladed knife around the edges of the dish to loosen the sides and dip the bottom briefly into hot water. Place an inverted platter on top of the dish and, grasping the platter and dish together firmly, turn them over. The headcheese should slide out of the dish easily.

Slice the headcheese thin and serve it with crackers or toast.

Crawfish Balls

To make about 3 dozen 1-inch balls

5 pounds live crawfish or ½ pound frozen crawfish meat, thoroughly defrosted and drained, and chopped into small bits
2 tablespoons butter
2 tablespoons flour
½ cup milk
¼ teaspoon ground hot red pepper (cayenne)
½ teaspoon salt

2 tablespoons finely chopped fresh parsley, preferably the flat-leaf Italian variety
2 tablespoons finely chopped scallions, including 3 inches of the green tops
3 eggs
3 cups soft fresh crumbs made from French- or Italian-type white bread, pulverized in a blender
Vegetable oil for deep frying

Crawfish are farmed commercially in Louisiana and are available there most of the year. During the summer, live crawfish also may be found in some Midwest and Pacific states, and purchased at gourmet fish markets or stores that specialize in Scandinavian foods. Frozen crawfish meat may be ordered from many fish dealers. Both live crawfish and the frozen meat can be obtained by mail (see Shopping Guide, page 150).

Soak the live crawfish in cold water for at least 10 minutes, then wash them thoroughly under cold running water. In a heavy 8- to 10-quart pot, bring 4 quarts of water to a boil over high heat. Using tongs, drop in the crawfish and boil them briskly, uncovered, for 5 minutes.

Drain the crawfish in a large colander and, when they are cool enough to handle, shell them one at a time in the following manner: With your hands, break off the ridged tail, snap it in half lengthwise and lift out the meat in one piece. If you like, you can snap off the large claws, break them with a nutcracker and pick out the bits of claw meat.

Some or all of the yellow fat or "butter" from the body of the crawfish may slide out when you break off the tail. If it does not, cut off the top of the head just behind the eyes, scoop the body shell clean with the tip of one thumb and pick out the yellow fat. Chop the crawfish meat into small bits, and reserve the meat and fat (there will be about 2 cups). Discard the shells, heads and intestinal matter. (Frozen crawfish meat needs only to be defrosted and drained, then chopped into small bits.)

In a heavy 1- to 1½-quart saucepan, melt the butter over moderate heat. Add the flour and mix well. Stirring constantly with a wire whisk, pour in the milk in a slow, thin stream and cook over high heat until the mixture comes to a boil, thickens heavily and is smooth. Reduce the heat to low and simmer uncovered for 2 or 3 minutes.

Stir in the red pepper and salt and, with a rubber spatula, scrape the entire contents of the pan into a deep bowl. Add the reserved crawfish meat and fat, the parsley and scallions, and mix all the ingredients together gently but thoroughly. Taste for seasoning.

Break the eggs into a shallow bowl and beat them to a froth with a fork or wire whisk. Spread the bread crumbs on a plate or a piece of wax paper. Scoop up about 1 tablespoonful of the crawfish mixture at a time and, with your hands, pat and shape it into a ball about 1 inch in diameter. As you form each ball, roll it in the bread crumbs, immerse it in the beaten eggs, then roll it in the crumbs again to coat it evenly. Arrange the balls side by side on wax paper and refrigerate them for at least 30 minutes to firm the coating.

Preheat the oven to its lowest setting. Line a large shallow baking pan with paper towels and place it in the middle of the oven.

Pour the oil into a deep fryer or large saucepan to a depth of 3 inches. Heat the oil to a temperature of 350° on a deep-frying thermometer.

Deep-fry the crawfish balls, five or six at a time, turning them with a slotted spoon for about 3 minutes, or until they are golden brown and crisp on all sides. As they brown, transfer the balls to the lined pan and keep them warm in the oven while you deep-fry the rest.

Serve the crawfish balls hot, as a first course or with drinks.

Daube Glacé
MOLDED JELLIED BEEF

To make two 9-by-5-by-3-inch
loaves

6 tablespoons vegetable oil
4 pounds beef shinbones, sawed
into 1-inch lengths
4 pounds veal shinbones, sawed into
1-inch lengths
3 medium-sized onions, peeled and
coarsely chopped
2 medium-sized celery stalks,
including the green leaves,
trimmed and coarsely chopped
2 large carrots, scraped and coarsely
chopped, plus 3 medium-sized
carrots, scraped and coarsely

grated
2 pounds fresh pigs' feet
3 sprigs fresh parsley
5 quarts water
5 pounds bottom round beef,
trimmed of excess fat and cut into
3 equal pieces
2 teaspoons finely chopped garlic
1 teaspoon ground hot red pepper
(cayenne) or 1 teaspoon freshly
ground black pepper
2 teaspoons salt
1 lemon, sliced crosswise into 6 thin
rounds

In a heavy 12-inch skillet, heat 4 tablespoons of the oil over moderate heat until a light haze forms above it. Brown the beef and veal bones in the hot oil, eight or nine pieces at a time, turning them frequently with tongs and regulating the heat so that the bones color deeply and evenly on all sides without burning. As they brown, transfer the bones to a heavy 10- to 12-quart stock pot.

Pour off all but about 2 tablespoons of the fat remaining in the skillet and in its place add the onions, celery and chopped carrots. Stirring frequently, cook over moderate heat for 8 to 10 minutes, or until the vegetables are soft and delicately brown. Scrape the vegetable mixture into the stock pot and drop in the pigs' feet and parsley. Add the water, bring to a boil over high heat, reduce the heat to low, and simmer partially covered for 4 hours.

With a slotted spoon, remove and discard the bones and pigs' feet. Strain the stock through a fine sieve into a large bowl, pressing down hard on the vegetables with the back of a spoon to extract all their juices before discarding the pulp. Set the stock aside.

Set the 12-inch skillet over moderate heat again and heat the remaining 2 tablespoons of oil. Brown the beef, one piece at a time, turning it with tongs and regulating the heat so that the meat colors richly and evenly on all sides without burning. As the pieces of beef brown, transfer them to a heavy 8- to 10-quart casserole.

Pour the reserved stock over the beef. The stock should cover the beef completely; add water if necessary. Bring to a boil over high heat, reduce the heat to low and cover the pot tightly. Simmer the beef for 3 to 3½ hours, or until it is very tender and shreds easily with a fork. Transfer the beef to a cutting board and strain the stock remaining in the casserole through a fine sieve lined with four layers of dampened cheesecloth and set over a large bowl.

When the beef is cool enough to handle, cut it into strips about ¼ inch wide and 2 inches long or, with the aid of two forks, pull the beef into 2-inch-long shreds. Drop the beef into a bowl, add the grated carrots, garlic, red or black pepper, and salt, and toss the ingredients together thoroughly with a fork. Refrigerate the beef mixture until you are ready to use it.

With a large spoon, skim the fat from the surface of the stock. Pour the stock into a 4- to 5-quart saucepan, cool to room temperature and refrigerate for at least 2 hours, or until the surface is covered with a layer of congealed fat. Carefully lift off the fat and discard it. Warm the stock over low heat and, when it liquefies, pour a ¼-inch layer of the stock into the bottoms of two 9-by-5-by-3-inch loaf pans. Refrigerate the pans until the stock has jelled and is firm to the touch.

(Keep the remaining stock at room temperature so that it remains liquid and ready to use. If it begins to set at any time, warm the stock briefly over low heat to soften it.)

Dip the lemon slices into the liquid stock and, when they are coated, arrange three of the slices in the bottom of each loaf pan. Chill until the lemon slices are anchored firmly.

Pour all the remaining liquid stock over the beef and mix well. Then ladle the mixture into the loaf pans, dividing it equally between them. Refrigerate the daube for at least 12 hours before serving.

Before unmolding the daube, scrape off any fat that has floated to the surface. Run a knife around the sides of one mold at a time and dip the bottom in hot water for a few seconds. Wipe the mold dry, place an inverted plate over it and, grasping plate and mold together firmly, turn them over. Rap the plate sharply on a table and the jellied beef should slide out easily. Refrigerate the *daube glacé* until ready to serve.

Oysters and Artichokes

To serve 6 as a first course

6 large artichokes, each 4 to 5 inches in diameter at the base
1 quart cold water combined with 2 tablespoons fresh lemon juice
1 dozen medium-sized oysters, shucked, with all their liquor reserved
3 tablespoons butter
¼ cup soft fresh crumbs made from French- or Italian-type bread with all the crusts removed and pulverized in a blender or finely shredded with a fork
1½ teaspoons finely chopped garlic
2 tablespoons paprika
1 cup chicken stock, fresh or canned
¼ cup cornstarch mixed with 3 tablespoons cold water
1 tablespoon strained fresh lemon juice
¼ teaspoon ground red pepper (cayenne)

Wash the artichokes under cold running water and bend and snap off the small bottom leaves and any bruised outer leaves. Then drop the artichokes into enough lightly salted boiling water to·cover them completely and cook briskly, uncovered, for 15 to 20 minutes, or until the bases show no resistance when pierced with the point of a small sharp knife.

With tongs, transfer the artichokes to a colander and invert them to drain. Cut off the stems flush with the bases of the artichokes, and drop the stems into a small bowl. Cut or pull off about two dozen of the large outside leaves of the artichokes and, with a spoon, scrape the soft pulp from each leaf into the bowl with the stems. (Discard the scraped leaves.) Using the back of a fork, mash the pulp and stems to a purée. There should be about ½ cup of purée; if necessary, pull off and scrape more leaves.

Cut or pull off the remaining green leaves of the artichokes, cover with foil or plastic wrap, and refrigerate until ready to serve. Following the diagrams on the opposite page, pull the thistlelike yellow leaves and hairy inner chokes away from the artichoke bottoms. Trim the surface of the artichoke bottoms, drop them into a bowl and pour the water-and-lemon-juice mixture over them. The liquid should cover the artichoke bottoms completely; if necessary, add more water. Set the bottoms aside.

About 15 minutes before you plan to serve the oysters and artichokes, drain the oysters and their liquor through a fine sieve lined with a double thickness of dampened cheesecloth and set over a bowl. Measure and reserve 1 cup of the oyster liquor. (If there is less than 1 cup, add fresh or bottled clam broth to make that amount.)

Pat the oysters dry with paper towels and cut them into quarters. Rinse the artichoke bottoms briefly under cold water, pat them dry with paper towels and cut them into ¼-inch dice. Reserve the oysters and artichoke-bottom dice in a bowl. In a heavy 6- to 8-inch skillet, melt 2 tablespoons of the butter over moderate heat, add the bread crumbs and stir until they are crisp and golden. Remove the pan from the heat and set aside.

Prepare the oyster-and-artichoke sauce in the following manner: In a 1- to 1½-quart enameled or stainless-steel saucepan, melt the remaining tablespoon of butter over moderate heat. When the foam begins to subside, add the garlic and stir for 1 minute. Add the paprika, then stir in the reserved artichoke purée, the oyster liquor and chicken stock. Stirring constantly with a wire whisk, bring to a boil over high heat. Reduce the heat to low, cover the pan partially and simmer for 10 minutes.

Transfer the entire contents of the saucepan to the jar of an electric blender and blend at high speed for about 30 seconds to reduce the mixture to a smooth purée. Return the purée to the saucepan and set over high heat. Give the cornstarch-and-water combination a quick stir to recombine it, then pour it slowly into the purée and whisk constantly until the mixture comes to a boil. Stir in the oysters and diced artichoke bottoms, reduce the heat to low and simmer for 2 or 3 minutes. When the oysters plump and their edges begin to curl, add the reserved bread crumbs, the lemon juice and the red pepper, and taste the sauce for seasoning.

To serve, ladle the sauce into six small bowls, dividing it evenly among them. Place each bowl in the center of a serving plate and arrange the chilled artichoke leaves attractively around it.

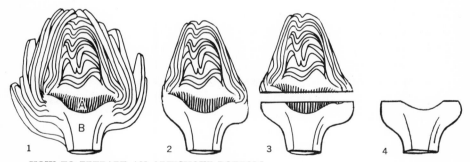

HOW TO PREPARE AN ARTICHOKE BOTTOM
Diced artichoke bottoms, like those incorporated into the oyster-and-artichoke sauce *(page 16),* are an elegant vegetable—but care must be taken in freeing a whole artichoke bottom for dicing. (1) The bottom (B) is below the hairy choke (A), as shown in this cross section. (2) Cut or pull off the green outside leaves. (3) Cut off the yellow thistlelike leaves (part of the choke will be removed along with them) and discard them. (4) Pull or cut off the remainder of the choke. Then trim the edges of the bottom, cutting away as little as possible, and peel off the tough outer skin of the stem end. (When artichoke bottoms are served whole the stem should be removed, but for a sauce the trimmed stem may be diced with the artichoke bottom.) Immerse the artichoke bottom in lemon juice and water to prevent discoloration and let it stand at room temperature until you are ready to dice and use it.

Oysters Roffignac

To serve 4

Rock salt

2 dozen large oysters, shucked, with all their liquor and the deeper halves of their shells reserved

1 pound uncooked shrimp

½ pound fresh mushrooms, trimmed, wiped with a dampened towel, and coarsely chopped

1 cup coarsely chopped onions

1 cup coarsely chopped scallions, including 3 inches of the green tops

4 teaspoons coarsely chopped garlic

½ pound butter, cut into ½-inch bits

¼ cup flour

½ cup dry red wine

¼ cup canned tomato purée

1½ teaspoons ground hot red pepper (cayenne)

1 teaspoon salt

Count Louis Philippe de Roffignac, for whom this dish is named, was mayor of New Orleans from 1820 to 1828.

Preheat the oven to 400°. Spread the rock salt to a depth of about ½ inch in four 8- to 9-inch pie pans. Arrange the pans on two large baking sheets and set them on the middle shelf of the oven to heat the salt while you prepare the oysters.

Drain the oysters and their liquor through a fine sieve lined with a double thickness of dampened cheesecloth and set over a bowl. Measure and reserve ½ cup of the oyster liquor. (If there is less than ½ cup, add enough water to make that amount.) Transfer the oysters to a bowl and set them aside. Scrub the oyster shells thoroughly with a stiff brush, then pat them dry with paper towels.

Shell the shrimp. Devein them by making a shallow incision down their backs with a small sharp knife and lifting out the black or white intestinal vein with the point of the knife. Wash the shrimp briefly in a sieve or colander set under cold running water and pat them completely dry with paper towels.

Put the shrimp, mushrooms, onions, scallions and garlic through the finest blade of a food grinder. In a heavy 10- to 12-inch skillet, melt the butter over moderate heat. When the foam begins to subside, add the ground shrimp mixture and, stirring frequently, cook for 4 to 5 minutes, until almost all the liquid that accumulates in the pan has evaporated.

Add the flour and mix well. Then, stirring constantly, gradually pour in the red wine, tomato purée and the reserved ½ cup of oyster liquor, and cook over moderate heat until the sauce comes to a boil, thickens heavily and is smooth. Reduce the heat to low and simmer for 2 or 3 minutes to remove the raw taste of the flour. Stir in the red pepper and salt, and taste for seasoning.

With a rubber spatula, scrape the entire contents of the skillet into the jar of an electric blender and blend at medium speed until the mixture is a smooth purée.

Arrange six oyster shells attractively in each of the salt-lined pans and place an oyster in each shell. Spoon the sauce over the oysters, dividing it equally among them. Bake in the middle of the oven for 15 minutes, or until the sauce is bubbly and the oysters begin to curl at the edges.

Serve the oysters Roffignac at once, directly from the baking pans.

NOTE: While the bed of salt helps to keep the shells from tipping and, if heated beforehand, will keep the oysters hot, it is not indispensable to the success of the dish. You may, if you like, bake the oysters in any shallow baking pan or pans large enough to hold the shells in one layer, and serve them from a heated platter.

Oysters Rockefeller
BAKED OYSTERS TOPPED WITH ANISE-FLAVORED GREEN SAUCE

To serve 4 as a first course

Rock salt
2 dozen large oysters, shucked, with all their liquor and the deeper halves of their shells reserved
Fresh or bottled clam broth
3 cups coarsely chopped scallions, including the green tops
3 cups coarsely chopped fresh parsley, preferably the flat-leaf Italian variety
1½ pounds fresh spinach, washed, trimmed, patted dry with paper towels and torn into 1-inch pieces
¾ pound unsalted butter, cut into ½-inch bits
4 teaspoons finely chopped garlic
¾ cup flour
3 tablespoons anchovy paste
¾ teaspoon ground hot red pepper (cayenne)
1½ teaspoons salt
¾ cup Herbsaint or Pernod

Oysters Rockefeller was created in 1899 by Jules Alciatore, the son and successor of M. Antoine Alciatore, who founded Antoine's Restaurant in 1840. It is told that he called the dish Rockefeller because the sauce was so rich. While Antoine's keeps its own recipe secret, there are many other versions. This one includes spinach in the green sauce.

Preheat the oven to 400°. Spread the rock salt to a depth of about ½ inch in four 8- or 9-inch pie pans. Arrange the pans on baking sheets and set them in the oven to heat the salt while you prepare the oysters.

Drain the oysters and their liquor through a fine sieve lined with a double thickness of dampened cheesecloth and set over a bowl. Measure and reserve 3 cups of the oyster liquor. (If there is less than 3 cups, add fresh or bottled clam broth to make up that amount.) Transfer the oysters to a bowl. Scrub the oyster shells, then pat them dry with paper towels.

Put the scallions, parsley and spinach through the finest blade of a meat grinder, and set aside. In a 2- to 3-quart enameled or stainless-steel saucepan, melt the butter over moderate heat, stirring so that it melts even-

Continued on next page

ly without browning. Add the garlic and stir for a minute or so, then add the flour and mix well. Stirring constantly with a wire whisk, pour in the 3 cups of oyster liquor in a slow, thin stream and cook over high heat until the sauce comes to a boil, thickens heavily and is smooth.

Stir in the anchovy paste, red pepper and salt. Then add the ground scallions, parsley and spinach, and reduce the heat to low. Stirring occasionally, simmer uncovered for 10 minutes, or until the sauce is thick enough to hold its shape almost solidly in the spoon. Remove the pan from the heat, stir in the Herbsaint or Pernod and taste for seasoning.

Arrange six oyster shells in each of the salt-lined pans and place an oyster in each shell. Spoon the sauce over the oysters, dividing it equally among them. Bake in the middle of the oven for 15 minutes, or until the sauce is delicately browned and the oysters begin to curl at the edges. Serve the oysters Rockefeller at once, directly from the baking pans.

NOTE: While the bed of salt helps to keep the shells from tipping and, if heated beforehand, will keep the oysters hot, it is not indispensable. You may, if you like, bake the oysters in any shallow pan large enough to hold the shells in one layer, and serve them from a heated platter.

Oysters Bienville

To serve 4

Rock salt
2 dozen large oysters, shucked, with all their liquor and the deeper halves of their shells reserved
1 pound uncooked shrimp
1½ pounds fresh mushrooms, trimmed, wiped with a dampened towel and coarsely chopped
6 slices bacon, coarsely chopped
½ cup coarsely chopped scallions, including 3 inches of the green tops
¼ cup coarsely chopped fresh

parsley, preferably the flat-leaf Italian variety
1 tablespoon coarsely chopped garlic
4 tablespoons butter
1 cup flour
½ cup American sauterne
2 cups milk
¼ cup strained fresh lemon juice
1½ teaspoons ground hot red pepper (cayenne)
1 teaspoon salt
4 egg yolks, lightly beaten
2 or 3 drops yellow food coloring (optional)

These richly sauced oysters were named in honor of Jean Baptiste le Moyne, Sieur de Bienville, the French colonial governor of Louisiana who founded New Orleans in 1718.

Preheat the oven to 400°. Spread the rock salt to a depth of about ½ inch in four 8- or 9-inch pie pans. Arrange the pans on two large baking sheets and set them on the middle shelf of the oven to heat the salt while you prepare the oysters.

Drain the oysters and their liquor through a fine sieve lined with a double thickness of dampened cheesecloth and set over a bowl. Measure and reserve 1½ cups of the oyster liquor. (If there is less than 1½ cups, add enough water to make that amount.) Transfer the oysters to a bowl and set them aside. Scrub the oyster shells thoroughly with a stiff brush, then pat them dry with paper towels.

Shell the shrimp. Devein them by making a shallow incision down their backs with a small sharp knife and lifting out the black or white intestinal vein with the point of the knife. Wash the shrimp briefly in a sieve or colander set under cold running water and pat them completely dry with paper towels.

Put the shrimp, mushrooms, bacon, scallions, parsley and garlic through the finest blade of a food grinder. In a heavy 10- to 12-inch skillet, melt the butter over moderate heat. When the foam begins to subside, add the shrimp mixture and, stirring frequently, cook for 4 to 5 minutes, until almost all of the liquid that accumulates in the pan has evaporated.

Add the flour and mix well. Then, stirring constantly, gradually pour in the sauterne, the milk and the reserved 1½ cups of oyster liquor, and cook over moderate heat until the sauce comes to a boil, thickens heavily and is smooth. Reduce the heat to low and simmer for 2 or 3 minutes to remove the raw taste of the flour.

Remove the skillet from the heat and stir in the lemon juice, red pepper and salt. Beat in the egg yolks and, if you wish, add 2 or 3 drops of yellow food coloring to give the sauce a brighter color. With a rubber spatula, scrape the entire contents of the skillet into the jar of an electric blender and blend at medium speed until the mixture is a smooth purée.

Arrange six oyster shells attractively in each of the salt-lined pans and place an oyster in each shell. Spoon the sauce over the oysters, dividing it equally among them. Bake in the middle of the oven for 15 minutes, or until the sauce is bubbly and the oysters begin to curl at the edges.

Serve the oysters Bienville at once, directly from the baking pans.

NOTE: While the bed of salt helps to keep the shells from tipping and, if heated beforehand, will keep the oysters hot, it is not indispensable to the success of the dish. You may, if you like, bake the oysters in any shallow baking pan or pans large enough to hold the shells in one layer, and serve them from a heated platter.

Oysters and Bacon en Brochette

To serve 6

14 tablespoons butter	3 dozen medium-sized shucked
6 slices homemade-type white bread,	oysters
trimmed of crusts and cut	1 teaspoon salt
diagonally into triangles	½ teaspoon freshly ground black
2 tablespoons finely chopped fresh	pepper
parsley, preferably the flat-leaf	2 cups unsifted corn flour (see
Italian variety	Glossary, page 150), or substitute
Vegetable oil for deep frying	2 cups all-purpose flour
8 slices bacon, cut crosswise into	1 lemon, cut lengthwise into 6
1-inch pieces	wedges

Preheat the oven to its lowest setting. At the same time, line two baking sheets with double thicknesses of paper towels and place them in the center of the oven.

In a heavy 8- to 10-inch skillet, melt 4 tablespoons of the butter over moderate heat. When the foam begins to subside, add four or five of the bread triangles and, turning them frequently with tongs, fry until they are crisp and golden brown on both sides. As they are toasted, transfer the bread triangles to one of the paper-lined pans to keep them warm. Then fry the rest of the triangles in a similar manner, adding up to 4 tablespoons more butter to the skillet as needed.

Add the remaining 6 tablespoons of butter to the same skillet, and stir so that it melts evenly without browning. Remove from the heat, stir in the parsley and set the skillet aside.

Pour the vegetable oil into a large deep fryer or a heavy saucepan at least 8 inches in diameter to a depth of 2 to 3 inches and heat the oil until it reaches a temperature of 350° on a deep-frying thermometer.

Place the bacon in a heavy 12-inch skillet and, stirring frequently, cook until the pieces are translucent but not brown. Set the bacon aside on paper towels to drain. Pat the oysters completely dry with paper towels and season them on both sides with the salt and pepper. One at a time, roll the oysters about on the flour to coat them evenly and vigorously shake off the excess flour.

String the pieces of bacon and the oysters alternately on six 6-inch-long metal skewers, pressing them tightly together. With tongs, carefully place two of the skewers in the hot oil and, turning the skewers frequently, deep-fry for 4 to 5 minutes, or until the oysters are plump and delicately browned. As they are cooked, transfer the oysters and bacon en brochette to the second paper-lined pan and keep them warm in the oven while you deep-fry the rest.

While the oysters are still hot, arrange two of the toast triangles on each of six heated serving plates and lay one skewer across them. Dribble the butter-and-parsley sauce over the oysters, garnish the plates with the lemon wedges and serve at once.

Red Bean Soup

To serve 8 to 10

4 to 5 quarts water
1 pound dried small red beans *(see Glossary, page 150)* or 1 pound dried red kidney beans
1½ pounds smoked ham hocks
2 medium-sized onions, peeled and coarsely chopped
1 cup coarsely chopped celery, including some of the leaves
1 large bay leaf, crumbled

Salt
Freshly ground black pepper
4 hard-cooked eggs, finely chopped
¼ cup dry red wine or red wine vinegar
2 scallions, including the green tops, trimmed and sliced crosswise into ¼-inch-thick rounds
2 lemons, sliced crosswise into ¼-inch-thick rounds

Bring 3½ quarts of water to a boil over high heat in a heavy 8- to 10-quart casserole. Drop in the beans and boil them for 2 minutes. Then turn off the heat and let the beans soak for 1 hour. Drain off the liquid, measure it and add enough fresh water to make up 3½ quarts. Return the liquid to the casserole, add the ham hocks, onions, celery and bay leaf, and bring to a boil over high heat. Reduce the heat to low and simmer, partially covered, for 3 hours, or until the ham is tender and shows no resistance when pierced deeply with the point of a small sharp knife.

Transfer the ham hocks to a plate and cut off and discard the skin and bones. Cut the meat into ¼-inch pieces. Purée the beans and vegetables and their cooking liquid through the medium blade of a food mill and return them to the casserole. Add the ham, taste the soup, and season it with salt and pepper.

Stir in the chopped eggs and bring the soup to a boil over high heat. Remove the casserole from the heat, stir in the wine or vinegar, and serve at once from a heated tureen or individual soup plates. Just before serving, garnish the soup with the scallions and lemon slices.

Turtle Soup

To serve 6

2 pounds fresh, frozen or canned
   turtle meat, thoroughly defrosted
   if frozen
2 quarts water
1 small onion, peeled and
   quartered, plus 1½ cups finely
   chopped onions
1 small bay leaf, crumbled
½ teaspoon ground hot red pepper
   (cayenne)
2 teaspoons salt

8 tablespoons butter, cut into
   ½-inch bits
½ cup flour
¼ cup canned tomato purée
¼ cup Worcestershire sauce
½ cup pale dry sherry
2 hard-cooked eggs, finely chopped
2 tablespoons finely chopped fresh
   parsley, preferably the flat-leaf
   Italian variety
1 lemon, sliced crosswise into
   ¼-inch-thick rounds

Combine the turtle meat and water in a heavy 5- to 6-quart casserole and bring to a boil over high heat, meanwhile skimming off the foam and scum as they rise to the surface. Drop in the quartered onion, bay leaf, red pepper and salt, and reduce the heat to low. Simmer, partially covered, for about 2 hours, or until the turtle meat is tender and shows no resistance when pierced with the point of a small sharp knife.

With a slotted spoon, transfer the meat to a plate and cut it into ½-inch cubes. Strain the contents of the casserole through a fine sieve set over a bowl and reserve 4 cups of the stock. (If there is less than 4 cups, add fresh or canned chicken stock to make up that amount.)

Rinse the casserole, add the butter bits and melt over moderate heat. When the foam subsides, add the chopped onions and, stirring frequently, cook for 8 to 10 minutes, or until they are soft and brown. Watch carefully and regulate the heat so that the onions color deeply without burning.

Mix in the flour and, still stirring occasionally, cook until the flour browns. Stirring constantly with a wire whisk, pour in the reserved 4 cups of stock and cook over high heat until the mixture comes to a boil, thickens lightly and is smooth.

Reduce the heat to low, stir in the tomato purée and Worcestershire sauce, and simmer uncovered for 10 minutes. Add the cubed turtle meat, the sherry and the chopped hard-cooked eggs and, stirring gently, simmer the soup for 2 or 3 minutes longer to heat the meat through. Add the parsley and taste for seasoning.

Ladle the soup into a heated tureen or individual soup plates, garnish with the lemon slices and serve at once.

24

Summer Fast-Day Soup

To serve 8 to 10

4 one-pound heads of iceberg
    lettuce
3 tablespoons butter
2 cups finely chopped onions
2 quarts water

3 pounds fresh peas, shelled, or
    substitute 3 cups frozen peas
2 teaspoons sugar
½ teaspoon salt
¼ cup finely cut fresh mint leaves

Days of fast and abstinence, when Roman Catholics eat no meat, have always tested the mettle of cooks. This soup is a favorite Lenten dish among the Roman Catholic families of New Orleans.

Wash the lettuce briefly under cold running water, remove the wilted outer leaves and cut each head into quarters. Shred the lettuce by first cutting out the cores and then slicing each of the quarters crosswise into ⅛-inch-wide strips.

In a heavy 6- to 8-quart casserole, melt the butter over moderate heat. Add the onions and, stirring frequently, cook for about 5 minutes, or until they are soft and translucent but not brown. Add the shredded lettuce, water, peas, sugar and salt and, still stirring, bring to a boil over high heat. Reduce the heat to low and simmer, partially covered, for 1½ hours, until all the vegetables are very soft.

Purée the entire contents of the casserole through the medium blade of a food mill and discard the coarse and stringy pulp. Return the vegetable purée to the casserole and stir over moderate heat until the soup comes to a simmer. Taste for seasoning.

Ladle the soup into a heated tureen or individual bowls and serve at once, garnished with the fresh mint. Or, if you prefer, cool the soup to room temperature, refrigerate it for at least 4 hours, and serve it chilled and garnished with the mint.

Oyster Soup

To serve 4

2 dozen medium-sized shucked
    oysters, with their liquor
Fish stock *(page 6)* or fresh or
    bottled clam broth
2 tablespoons butter
⅓ cup finely chopped celery
¼ cup finely chopped scallions,
    including 3 inches of the green

tops
1 tablespoon flour
¼ teaspoon salt
⅛ teaspoon ground hot red pepper
    (cayenne)
2 egg yolks
1 tablespoon finely chopped fresh
    parsley, preferably the flat-leaf
    Italian variety

Drain the oysters through a fine sieve set over a bowl, reserving all their liquor. Pat the oysters completely dry with paper towels, cut each of them into thirds and set aside. Measure the liquor and add enough fish stock or clam broth to make 2 cups.

In a heavy 2- to 3-quart saucepan, melt the butter over moderate heat. When the foam begins to subside, add the celery and scallions and, stirring frequently, cook for about 5 minutes, or until the vegetables are soft but not brown. Add the flour and mix well. Stirring constantly with a wire whisk, pour in the reserved 2 cups of oyster liquor in a slow, thin stream and cook over high heat until the sauce comes to a boil, thickens lightly and is smooth.

Reduce the heat to low, add the oysters, salt and red pepper, and simmer uncovered for 2 to 3 minutes, or until the oysters plump up. In a small bowl, beat the egg yolks with a fork or wire whisk. When they are smooth, ladle in about 2 tablespoons of the simmering liquid and mix well. Then, stirring constantly, pour the heated egg yolks gradually into the soup. Still stirring, cook over low heat for 2 to 3 minutes longer, until the soup thickens heavily. Do not let the soup come anywhere near a boil or the egg yolks will curdle.

Taste for seasoning, stir in the parsley and serve the oyster soup at once from a heated tureen or individual soup plates.

Squirrel-and-Oyster Gumbo

To serve 6

2 dozen medium-sized oysters, shucked, with all their liquor reserved
4 to 5 cups water
1½ pounds squirrel meat, cut into 6 serving pieces
½ teaspoon salt
¼ teaspoon freshly ground black pepper
¼ cup flour
¼ cup vegetable oil
6 tablespoons brown *roux (page 3)*
½ cup finely chopped onions
½ cup finely chopped scallions, including 3 inches of the green tops
½ pound lean boneless fully

cooked smoked ham, cut into ¼-inch cubes
1 dried hot red chili, about 1½ inches long, washed, stemmed, seeded and finely chopped *(caution: see note, page 6)*
¼ teaspoon ground hot red pepper (cayenne)
¼ teaspoon crumbled dried thyme
1 medium-sized bay leaf, crumbled
¼ cup finely chopped fresh parsley, preferably the flat-leaf Italian variety
2 teaspoons filé powder *(see Glossary, page 150)*
6 cups freshly cooked long-grain white rice

Drain the oysters through a fine sieve set over a bowl. Set the oysters aside, then measure the oyster liquor into a saucepan and add enough water to make 6 cups. Bring the liquid to a boil over high heat, remove the pan from the heat and cover to keep it warm.

Pat the pieces of squirrel dry with paper towels and season them with the salt and pepper. One at a time, turn the pieces about in the flour to coat them lightly on all sides and vigorously shake off the excess flour.

In a heavy 12-inch skillet, heat the oil over high heat until a light haze forms above it. Brown the pieces of squirrel in the hot oil, turning them frequently with tongs and regulating the heat so that they color richly and evenly without burning. As they brown, transfer the pieces to a plate.

Stirring constantly, warm the brown *roux* in a heavy 4- to 5-quart casserole set over low heat. Add the onions and scallions and, stirring frequently, cook over moderate heat until the vegetables are soft but not brown. Add the ham and turn it about with a spoon to mix it in well. Then, stirring constantly, pour in the warm oyster-liquor mixture in a slow, thin stream. Add the pieces of squirrel and the liquid that has accumulated around them, the chili, red pepper, thyme and bay leaf.

Bring to a boil over high heat, stirring constantly, then reduce the heat to low and partially cover the casserole. Simmer the stew for 1½ to 2 hours, or until the squirrel is tender and shows no resistance when pierced deeply with the point of a small sharp knife.

Continued on next page

Add the reserved oysters and simmer for 4 to 5 minutes longer, or until the oysters plump up and their edges begin to curl. Remove the pot from the heat and immediately stir in the parsley and 2 teaspoons of filé powder. Taste for seasoning; the gumbo should be hotly spiced and may require more red pepper.

Ladle the gumbo into a heated tureen and serve at once, accompanied by the rice in a separate bowl. Traditionally, a cupful of the rice is mounded in a heated soup plate and the gumbo spooned around it. Present additional filé powder for those who prefer gumbo with a stronger flavor.

Duck-and-Sausage Gumbo

To serve 6 to 8

1 pound *chaurice (page 84)* or other hot sausage, skinned and sliced into ½-inch-thick rounds	1 cup finely chopped celery
	1 cup finely chopped green peppers
Vegetable oil, if needed	3 quarts warm water
2 five-pound ducks, each cut into 8 pieces	½ teaspoon Tabasco sauce
	1½ teaspoons ground hot red pepper (cayenne)
4 teaspoons salt	¼ cup finely chopped fresh parsley, preferably the flat-leaf Italian variety
Freshly ground black pepper	
½ cup flour	
6 tablespoons brown *roux (page 3)*	Filé powder *(see Glossary, page 150)*
1 cup finely chopped onions	6 to 8 cups freshly cooked long-grain white rice
½ cup finely chopped scallions	

In a heavy ungreased 12-inch skillet, fry the sausage over low heat, turning the slices frequently with a slotted spatula until the bottom of the pan is filmed with fat. Increase the heat to moderate and, turning the slices occasionally, continue to fry until the sausage is richly browned. Transfer the sausage slices to paper towels to drain. There should be about ½ cup of fat in the skillet; if not, add vegetable oil to make up that amount.

Pat the pieces of duck completely dry with paper towels and remove any large pieces of fat. Season the birds with 2 teaspoons of the salt and a few grindings of black pepper. Roll the ducks in the flour to coat the pieces on all sides and vigorously shake off the excess flour.

Brown the ducks, five or six pieces at a time, in the hot fat remaining in the skillet. Turn the pieces frequently with tongs and regulate the heat so that they color deeply and evenly without burning. As they brown, transfer the pieces of duck to paper towels to drain.

Warm the *roux* over low heat in a heavy 12-quart enameled or cast-iron pot. When the *roux* is smooth and fluid, stir in the onions, scallions and celery. Stirring frequently, cook over moderate heat for about 5 minutes, or until the vegetables are soft. Mix in the green peppers. Then, stirring constantly, pour in the warm water in a slow, thin stream and bring to a boil over high heat.

Add the sausage slices, the pieces of duck, the remaining 2 teaspoons of salt, the Tabasco and the red pepper. When the mixture returns to a boil, reduce the heat to low and cover the pot partially. Simmer the gumbo for 2 hours. Remove the pot from the heat and, with a large spoon, skim as much fat from the surface as possible. Stir in the parsley and 2 teaspoons of filé powder, and taste for seasoning. The gumbo should be hotly spiced and may require more Tabasco and/or red pepper.

Ladle the gumbo into a heated tureen and serve at once, accompanied by the rice in a separate bowl. Traditionally, a cupful of the rice is mounded in a heated soup plate and the gumbo spooned around it. Present additional filé powder for those who like gumbo with a stronger flavor.

Gumbo z'Herbes

To serve 10

1 pound fresh collard or mustard
   greens
1 pound fresh spinach
1 pound beet or turnip greens
½ pound chicory
1 pound green cabbage leaves
1 large bunch fresh watercress
1 large bunch fresh parsley plus
   1 tablespoon finely chopped fresh
   parsley, both preferably the flat-
   leaf Italian variety
The tops of 6 large carrots
The tops of a large bunch of
   radishes
4 quarts water
3 tablespoons vegetable shortening
1 pound cooked lean smoked ham,
   sliced ¼ inch thick and cut into

¼-inch cubes
1 pound lean boneless veal,
   trimmed of excess fat, sliced
   ¼ inch thick and cut into
   ¼-inch cubes
1 cup finely chopped onions
1 cup coarsely chopped scallions,
   including the green tops
2 medium-sized bay leaves, finely
   crumbled
2 whole cloves
1 teaspoon crumbled dried thyme
¼ teaspoon ground allspice
½ teaspoon ground hot red pepper
   (cayenne)
¼ teaspoon freshly ground black
   pepper
1½ teaspoons salt

Originally gumbo z'herbes (a Creole contraction for gumbo aux herbes) was a Lenten dish that included no meat but was always made with at least seven different kinds of greens or herbs. In recent years gumbo z'herbes has come to be served all through the year, and is often made with ham and veal, as in this recipe.

With a sharp knife, trim away any bruised or blemished spots on the collard or mustard greens, spinach, the beet or turnip greens, chicory, cabbage

Continued on next page

leaves, watercress, the bunch of parsley and the tops of the carrots and radishes. Wash all the leaves in several changes of cold running water to remove any traces of dirt or sand.

In a heavy 10- to 12-quart pot, bring the water to a boil over high heat and drop in the greens by the handful. When the water returns to a boil, reduce the heat to low and simmer, partially covered, for 2 hours.

Strain the greens, a cup or so at a time, through a fine sieve set over a bowl, pressing down hard on the greens with the back of a large spoon to extract all their juices. There should be about 6 cups of liquid; if necessary add water. As you proceed, put the pulp of the greens through the medium blade of a food grinder and reserve it. Set the pot aside.

Melt the shortening over moderate heat in a heavy 12-inch skillet. Drop in the ham and veal cubes and, stirring frequently, brown the meats lightly. Add the onions, scallions and the tablespoon of chopped parsley and, still stirring, cook for about 5 minutes, or until the onions are soft and translucent but not brown. Add the ground greens and simmer uncovered over low heat for 15 minutes.

With a rubber spatula, scrape the entire contents of the skillet into the original stock pot. Add the reserved 6 cups of cooking liquid, the bay leaves, cloves, thyme, allspice, red and black pepper, and salt, and mix well. Bring to a boil over high heat, reduce the heat to low and cover tightly. Then simmer the *gumbo z'herbes* for 1 hour longer. Taste for seasoning and serve at once from a heated tureen or individual soup plates.

Crab, Shrimp and Okra Gumbo

To serve 4

1 pound uncooked medium-sized shrimp (about 20 to 24 to the pound)
7 quarts water
5 dried hot red chilies, each about 2 inches long *(caution: see note, page 6)*
1 lemon, cut crosswise into ¼-inch-thick slices
3 large bay leaves
1½ teaspoons crumbled, dried thyme
1 tablespoon plus 1 teaspoon salt
10 live blue crabs, each about 8 ounces
4 tablespoons brown *roux (page 3)*
½ cup coarsely chopped onions
1½ teaspoons finely chopped garlic
½ pound fresh okra, trimmed, washed and cut into 1-inch chunks
¾ cup coarsely chopped green pepper
1 teaspoon ground hot red pepper (cayenne)
½ teaspoon Tabasco sauce
4 to 6 cups freshly cooked long-grain white rice

Shell the shrimp. Devein them by making a shallow incision down their backs with a small knife and lifting out the intestinal vein with the point of the knife. Wash the shrimp briefly and set them aside.

In a 10- to 12-quart pot, bring the water, chilies, lemon slices, 2 bay leaves, 1 teaspoon of thyme and 1 tablespoon of salt to a boil over high heat. Drop in the crabs and boil briskly, uncovered, for 5 minutes. Remove the crabs from the stock with tongs, and set them aside to cool.

Drop the shrimp into the stock remaining in the pot and cook uncovered for 3 to 5 minutes, or until they are pink and firm to the touch. With tongs, transfer the shrimp to a plate. Then boil the stock, uncovered, until it is reduced to 3 quarts. Strain the stock through a fine sieve set over a large pot, and discard the seasonings. Cover the pot to keep the stock warm until you are ready to use it.

When the crabs are cool enough to handle, shell them in the following fashion: Grasping the body of the crab firmly in one hand, break off the large claws and legs close to the body. With the point of a small sharp knife, pry off the pointed shell, or apron, and loosen the large bottom shell from around the meat and cartilage, cutting near the edges where the legs are joined to the shell. Lift the body of the crab, break it in half lengthwise, then with the knife pick out the firm white pieces of meat. Discard the gray featherlike gills and tough bits of cartilage but save the morsels of yellow liver and "fat" as well as any pieces of orange roe. Leave the large claws in their shells, but crack the legs lengthwise with a cleaver and pick out the meat. Reserve the meat, claws and roe (if any).

In a heavy 5- to 6-quart casserole, warm the *roux* over low heat, stirring constantly. Add the onions and garlic and stir for about 5 minutes, or until they are soft. Add the okra and green peppers and mix well.

Stirring constantly, pour in the reserved warm stock in a slow, thin stream and bring to a boil over high heat. (If the stock has cooled, reheat before adding it.) Add the red pepper, Tabasco, the remaining bay leaf, ½ teaspoon of thyme and 1 teaspoon of salt. Stir in the crabmeat and claws, reduce the heat to low and simmer, partially covered, for 1 hour.

Add the shrimp and simmer a few minutes longer, then taste for seasoning. The gumbo may require more Tabasco or red pepper.

Ladle the gumbo into a heated tureen and serve at once, accompanied by the rice in a separate bowl. Traditionally, a cupful of rice is mounded in a heated soup plate and the gumbo spooned around it. Give each diner a nutcracker so that the claws can be cracked easily at the table.

Crawfish Bisque

To serve 6

7½ pounds live crawfish
6 quarts water
2 cups coarsely chopped onions plus 3 cups finely chopped onions
6 fresh parsley sprigs plus ¼ cup finely chopped fresh parsley, preferably the flat-leaf Italian variety
1 large bay leaf, crumbled
¼ teaspoon crumbled dried thyme
6 whole black peppercorns
6 tablespoons brown *roux* (*page 3*)
1 cup finely chopped celery
2 tablespoons plus 2 teaspoons finely chopped garlic

A 1-pound can tomatoes, drained and coarsely chopped
1 tablespoon canned tomato paste
3 teaspoons salt
14 tablespoons butter
2 cups soft fresh bread crumbs made from French- or Italian-type white bread, pulverized in a blender
1 cup finely chopped scallions, including 3 inches of the green tops
1 teaspoon ground hot red pepper (cayenne)
4 eggs, lightly beaten
2 cups flour
Vegetable oil for deep frying

Soak the live crawfish in cold water for at least 10 minutes, then thoroughly wash them, a small batch at a time, in a colander set under cold running water. Combine the water, the 2 cups of coarsely chopped onions, 3 of the parsley sprigs, the bay leaf, thyme and peppercorns in a heavy 8- to 10-quart pot and bring to a boil over high heat. Using tongs, drop in the crawfish and boil them briskly, uncovered, for 5 minutes.

With the tongs or a slotted spoon, transfer the crawfish to paper towels to drain. Then boil the liquid remaining in the pot over high heat until it is reduced to about 2 quarts. Strain the stock through a fine sieve lined with a double layer of dampened cheesecloth and set over a saucepan. Reserve 6 cups of the stock, and discard the vegetables and seasonings.

When the crawfish are cool enough to handle, shell them one at a time in the following manner: With your hands, break off the ridged tail, snap it in half lengthwise and lift out the meat in one piece. Set the meat aside, but discard the tail shell. Some or all of the yellow fat, or "butter," from the body of the crawfish may slide out when you break off the tail. If it does, reserve it.

Snap off the large claws and the smaller legs of the crawfish and—if you like—break the claws with a nutcracker and pick out the bits of meat. Discard the claw shells and legs. Cut off the top of the head just behind the eyes and discard. Then scoop the body shell clean with the tip of a finger or thumb and pick out any fat. Set this shell and all the fat aside, and discard the intestinal matter.

Put all of the crawfish meat and fat through the finest blade of a food grinder, or chop it as fine as possible. There should be about 3 cups of the ground meat. Reserve the meat and 48 of the crawfish body shells, which in Louisiana are referred to as crawfish "heads."

To prepare the bisque, bring the reserved 6 cups of crawfish stock to a boil over high heat. Remove the pan from the heat and cover tightly to keep the stock hot.

In a heavy 6- to 8-quart casserole, warm the brown *roux* over low heat for 2 or 3 minutes, stirring it all the while. Add 2 cups of the finely chopped onions, the celery and 2 tablespoons of the garlic. Stirring frequently, cook over moderate heat for about 5 minutes, or until the vegetables are soft but not brown.

Stir in the tomatoes, tomato paste, the 3 remaining parsley sprigs and 2 teaspoons of the salt. Stirring constantly, pour in the hot stock in a slow, thin stream and bring to a simmer over moderate heat. Immediately reduce the heat to low and simmer, partially covered, for 45 minutes.

Strain the entire contents of the casserole through a fine sieve set over a deep pot, pressing down hard on the vegetables and seasonings with the back of a large spoon to extract all their juices before discarding the pulp. Then return the crawfish bisque to the casserole.

Meanwhile, prepare the stuffed crawfish "heads" in the following manner: In a heavy 12-inch skillet, melt 6 tablespoons of the butter over moderate heat. When the foam begins to subside, add the bread crumbs and, stirring frequently, fry them until they are crisp and golden brown. With a rubber spatula, scrape the crumbs into a deep bowl and set them aside.

Add the remaining 8 tablespoons of butter to the skillet and melt over moderate heat. Drop in the remaining cup of finely chopped onions, the scallions and the remaining 2 teaspoons of garlic and, stirring frequently, cook for about 5 minutes, or until the vegetables are soft but not brown.

Scrape the contents of the skillet into the bowl of toasted bread crumbs. Add 2 cups of ground crawfish meat, the ¼ cup of chopped parsley, ½ teaspoon of the red pepper and the remaining teaspoon of salt, and mix the stuffing ingredients together gently but thoroughly.

For each stuffed crawfish head, scoop up about 1 tablespoonful of the stuffing and pack it tightly into one of the reserved shells. Immerse each head in the beaten eggs and turn it about in the flour to coat it evenly. As you proceed, set the stuffed heads aside on a platter or wax paper.

Preheat the oven to its lowest setting, then line a large shallow baking dish with a double thickness of paper towels and set it on the middle shelf of the oven.

Pour vegetable oil into a deep fryer or large heavy saucepan to a depth of 2 to 3 inches and heat the oil until it reaches a temperature of 350° on a deep-frying thermometer.

Deep-fry the coated stuffed crawfish heads, seven or eight at a time, turning them about with a slotted spoon until they are golden brown on all sides. As they are fried, transfer them to the paper-lined dish and keep them warm in the oven until you are ready to serve them.

Continued on next page

Shortly before you plan to serve the bisque, bring it to a simmer over moderate heat. Stir in the remaining cup of ground crawfish meat and ½ teaspoon of red pepper and simmer, partially covered, for about 15 minutes. Taste for seasoning.

Ladle the bisque into a large heated tureen or individual soup plates and, just before serving, drop in the crawfish heads.

Cold Shrimp-and-Tomato Bisque

To serve 4 to 6

1 pound raw shrimp	1 cup light cream
3 cups water	1½ teaspoons salt
2 tablespoons butter	¼ teaspoon ground hot red pepper
¼ cup finely chopped onions	(cayenne)
3 tablespoons flour	1 large firm ripe tomato, washed,
1 tablespoon canned tomato purée	stemmed, and sliced crosswise
2 teaspoons curry powder	into ¼-inch-thick rounds
	2 hard-cooked eggs, finely chopped

Shell the shrimp. Devein them by making a shallow incision down their backs with a small sharp knife and lifting out the black or white intestinal vein with the point of the knife. Wash the shrimp briefly in a sieve or colander set under cold running water.

Bring the 3 cups of water to a boil over high heat, drop in the shrimp and cook briskly, uncovered, for 3 to 5 minutes, or until they are pink and firm to the touch. With a slotted spoon, transfer the shrimp to a bowl and put them through the finest blade of a food grinder. Set the shrimp aside and reserve the cooking liquid.

In a heavy 2- to 3-quart saucepan, melt the butter over moderate heat. When the foam begins to subside, add the onions and, stirring frequently, cook for about 5 minutes, or until they are soft and translucent but not brown. Add the flour, tomato purée and curry powder, and mix well. Stirring constantly with a wire whisk, pour in the reserved cooking liquid in a slow, thin stream and cook over high heat until the sauce comes to a boil, thickens lightly and is smooth.

Reduce the heat to low and simmer for 3 or 4 minutes to remove the raw taste of flour. Add the ground shrimp, cream, salt and red pepper, and stir over moderate heat until the soup comes to a boil. Taste for seasoning, pour the soup into a bowl, and let it cool to room temperature. Cover the bowl tightly with foil or plastic wrap and refrigerate the soup for at least 4 hours, until it is thoroughly chilled.

To serve, ladle the soup into chilled individual bowls and garnish each portion with the sliced tomato and chopped eggs.

Crab-and-Shrimp Bouillon

To serve 6 to 8

1 pound raw shrimp
2 quarts fish stock *(page 6)*
2 tablespoons butter
½ cup finely chopped onions
½ cup finely chopped celery
1 teaspoon finely chopped garlic
½ pound fresh, canned or frozen

crabmeat, thoroughly drained and
picked over to remove all bits of
shell and cartilage
½ teaspoon crumbled dried thyme
1 small bay leaf
½ teaspoon ground hot red pepper
(cayenne)

Shell the shrimp. Devein them by making a shallow incision down their backs with a small sharp knife and lifting out the black or white intestinal vein with the point of the knife. Wash the shrimp briefly in a sieve or colander set under cold running water.

Bring the fish stock to a boil in a heavy 3- to 4-quart saucepan set over high heat. Drop in the shrimp and cook briskly, uncovered, for 3 to 5 minutes, or until they are pink and firm to the touch. With a slotted spoon, transfer the shrimp to a bowl and put them through the medium blade of a food grinder. Set the ground shrimp aside and reserve all of the cooking liquid.

In a heavy 4- to 6-quart casserole, melt the butter over moderate heat. When the foam begins to subside, add the onions, celery and garlic and, stirring frequently, cook for about 5 minutes, or until the vegetables are soft but not brown. Pour in the reserved cooking liquid, then add the ground shrimp, the crabmeat, thyme, bay leaf and red pepper, and bring the soup to a boil over high heat. Reduce the heat to low and simmer for 2 or 3 minutes.

Pick out and discard the bay leaf. Taste for seasoning and serve the crab-and-shrimp bouillon at once from a heated tureen or from heated individual soup plates.

Eggs Hussarde
POACHED EGGS, CANADIAN BACON AND TOMATO
ON RUSKS WITH MARCHAND DE VIN AND HOLLANDAISE SAUCES

To serve 4

3 tablespoons butter
4 slices Canadian bacon
4 Holland rusks
½ cup *marchand de vin* sauce
    (opposite)
1 large firm ripe tomato, washed,

stemmed and cut crosswise into
    four ¼-inch-thick rounds
4 large very fresh eggs
½ cup freshly made hollandaise
    sauce *(page 5)*
Paprika

Preheat the oven to 250°. In a heavy 12-inch skillet, melt the butter over moderate heat. When the foam begins to subside, add the bacon. Turn the slices frequently with tongs and regulate the heat so that they color richly and evenly on both sides without burning.

As they brown, place the bacon slices on top of the Holland rusks. Remove the skillet from the heat and reserve it. Place the rusks on four individual heatproof serving plates and ladle the *marchand de vin* sauce over the bacon, dividing it equally among the slices. Set the plates in the oven to keep the bacon and sauce warm.

Add the tomato slices to the fat remaining in the skillet and, turning them frequently with a wide metal spatula, cook over moderate heat until the slices are golden brown on both sides. Place the tomato slices in one layer in a separate shallow baking dish and set them in the oven.

To poach the eggs, pour cold water into a 10- to 12-inch skillet to a depth of about 2 inches. Bring to a simmer, then reduce the heat so that the surface of the liquid barely shimmers. Break the eggs into individual saucers. Gently slide one egg from its saucer into the water and, with a large spoon, lift the white over the yolk. Repeat once or twice more to enclose the yolk completely in the white.

One at a time, slide the three other eggs from the saucers into the pan, enclosing them in their whites and spacing them at least 1 inch apart. Poach the eggs for 3 or 4 minutes, until the whites are set and the yolks feel soft when prodded gently.

With a slotted spatula transfer the poached eggs to a large bowl half-filled with lukewarm water and set them aside while you prepare the hollandaise sauce.

Before assembling the eggs *hussarde,* transfer the poached eggs to a linen towel with a slotted spatula and let them drain briefly.

Place a tomato slice on each of the sauced, ham-topped rusks and carefully place the poached eggs on the tomatoes. Ladle about 2 tablespoons of the hollandaise sauce over each egg and sprinkle the tops lightly with the paprika. Serve at once.

Marchand de Vin Sauce

To make about 1½ cups

8 tablespoons butter
½ cup finely chopped scallions, including 3 inches of the green tops
¼ cup finely chopped onions
2 teaspoons finely chopped garlic
1 cup finely chopped fresh mushrooms

2 tablespoons flour
½ cup finely chopped lean cooked smoked ham
1 cup chicken stock, fresh or canned
½ cup dry red wine
Salt (optional)
Freshly ground black pepper (optional)

In a heavy 8- to 10-inch skillet, melt the butter over moderate heat. When the foam subsides, add the scallions, onions and garlic and, stirring frequently, cook for about 5 minutes, or until they are soft but not brown.

Add the mushrooms and, still stirring from time to time, cook for about 5 minutes longer, or until they are soft and almost all of the liquid that accumulates in the pan has evaporated. Add the flour and mix well. Then stir in the ham.

Stirring constantly with a wire whisk, pour in the chicken stock and wine in slow, thin streams and cook over high heat until the sauce comes to a boil, thickens lightly and is smooth. Reduce the heat to low and simmer for 2 or 3 minutes longer to remove the raw taste of the flour. Then taste and add salt and pepper if you wish.

Creole Shrimp Omelets

To make 4 omelets

SAUCE

¼ cup olive oil
1 cup finely chopped onions
1 cup finely chopped celery
½ cup finely chopped green
    peppers
2 teaspoons finely chopped garlic
A 1-pound can tomatoes, drained
    and coarsely chopped, with their

liquid reserved
2 tablespoons finely chopped fresh
    parsley, preferably the flat-leaf
    Italian variety
1 medium-sized bay leaf
¼ teaspoon crumbled dried thyme
¼ teaspoon ground hot red pepper
    (cayenne)
1 teaspoon salt

First prepare the sauce in the following manner: In a heavy 10- to 12-inch skillet, heat the olive oil over moderate heat until a light haze forms above it. Add the onions, celery, green peppers and garlic and, stirring frequently, cook for about 5 minutes, or until they are soft but not brown. Stir in the coarsely chopped tomatoes and their liquid, 2 tablespoons of parsley, the bay leaf, thyme, red pepper and 1 teaspoon of salt. Bring to a boil over high heat, reduce the heat to low and simmer, tightly covered, for 20 minutes. Remove the skillet from the heat and discard the bay leaf. Taste for seasoning, then set the sauce aside in the skillet.

FILLING

½ pound uncooked shrimp
4 tablespoons butter
½ cup finely chopped scallions,
    including 3 inches of the green
    tops
½ cup finely chopped drained

canned tomatoes
2 tablespoons finely chopped fresh
    parsley, preferably the flat-leaf
    Italian variety
⅛ teaspoon ground white pepper
1 teaspoon salt

Meanwhile, shell the shrimp. Devein them by making a shallow incision down their backs with a small sharp knife and lifting out the black or white intestinal vein with the point of the knife. Wash the shrimp briefly in a colander set under cold running water and pat them completely dry with paper towels. Chop the shrimp into small bits.

To make the filling, melt 4 tablespoons of butter in a heavy 1- to 1½-quart saucepan set over moderate heat. When the foam begins to subside, add the shrimp and scallions and stir for 2 to 3 minutes, or until the shrimp are pink and the scallions are soft. Add the finely chopped tomatoes, 2 tablespoons of parsley, the white pepper and 1 teaspoon of salt. Stirring constantly, cook briskly over high heat until all of the liquid in the pan has evaporated. Taste the filling for seasoning and set the pan aside off the heat.

OMELETS

12 eggs	Freshly ground black pepper
Salt	4 tablespoons butter

For each omelet, break three eggs into a small bowl, season with a little salt and a few grindings of black pepper, and stir briskly with a table fork for 20 to 30 seconds, or until the whites and yolks are blended together. Heat an ungreased 7- to 8-inch omelet pan until it is very hot, drop in 1 tablespoon of butter and swirl it in the pan so that it melts quickly and coats the bottom and sides. When the foam begins to subside but before the butter browns, pour in the eggs.

Working quickly, stir the eggs with the flat of the fork, at the same time shaking the pan back and forth vigorously to prevent the eggs from sticking. In a few seconds, the eggs will form a film on the bottom of the pan and the top will thicken to a light, curded custard. Still shaking the pan with one hand, gently stir through the top custard to spread the still-liquid eggs into the firmer areas; try not to pierce the bottom film.

Spoon about ¼ cup of the filling in a band down the center of the omelet. Then lift the edge closest to you with the fork and gently fold the omelet in half. Let it rest for a moment on the lip of the pan, then tilt the pan and roll the omelet out onto a heated plate. Immediately wipe the pan clean and prepare three more omelets in the same fashion.

Reheat the reserved sauce briefly and ladle it over the filled omelets, dividing the sauce equally among them. Serve at once.

Eggs Sardou

POACHED EGGS WITH ARTICHOKE BOTTOMS AND CREAMED SPINACH

To serve 4 or 8

6 tablespoons butter	1 teaspoon salt
2 tablespoons flour	¼ teaspoon ground white pepper
1 cup milk	8 canned artichoke bottoms, drained
1½ pounds fresh spinach, cooked, drained, squeezed dry and finely chopped (about 2 cups)	8 very fresh eggs
	1 cup freshly made hollandaise sauce (page 5)

In a heavy 1- to 2-quart saucepan, melt 2 tablespoons of the butter over moderate heat. When the foam begins to subside, add the flour and mix well. Stirring constantly with a wire whisk, pour in the milk in a slow, thin stream and cook over high heat until the sauce comes to a boil, thickens lightly and is smooth. Reduce the heat to low and simmer for about 3

Continued on next page

minutes to remove any raw taste of the flour. Then stir in the spinach, ½ teaspoon of the salt and the white pepper. Taste for seasoning, remove the pan from the heat and cover tightly.

Melt the remaining 4 tablespoons of butter in a heavy 10- to 12-inch skillet. Add the artichoke bottoms, concave side down, and baste them with the hot butter. Sprinkle them with the remaining ½ teaspoon of salt, reduce the heat to the lowest possible point, cover tightly and cook for several minutes until the artichoke bottoms are heated through. Do not let them brown. Remove the skillet from the heat and cover tightly to keep the artichoke bottoms warm.

To poach the eggs, pour cold water into a 12-inch skillet to a depth of about 2 inches. Bring to a simmer, then reduce the heat so that the surface of the liquid barely shimmers. Break the eggs into individual saucers. Gently slide one of the eggs from its saucer into the water, and with a large spoon, lift the white over the yolk. Repeat once or twice more to enclose the yolk completely in the white.

One at a time, slide the seven other eggs into the pan, enclosing them in their whites and spacing them about an inch apart. Poach the eggs for 3 or 4 minutes, until the whites are set and the yolks feel soft when prodded gently. With a slotted spatula, transfer the poached eggs to a large bowl half-filled with lukewarm water and set them aside while you prepare the hollandaise sauce.

Before assembling the eggs Sardou, transfer the poached eggs to a linen towel with a slotted spatula to drain briefly. If the creamed spinach and artichoke bottoms have cooled, warm them over low heat.

Spread the creamed spinach smoothly on a heated serving platter to make a bed about ¼ inch deep. Arrange the artichoke bottoms, concave sides up, on the spinach and place an egg in each one. Spoon the hollandaise sauce over the eggs and serve at once.

Eggs Nouvelle Orléans
POACHED EGGS AND CRABMEAT WITH BRANDIED CREAM SAUCE

To serve 4

SAUCE

3 tablespoons butter	1 teaspoon strained fresh lemon
2 tablespoons finely chopped onions	juice
3 tablespoons flour	⅛ teaspoon ground hot red pepper
1½ cups milk	(cayenne)
2 tablespoons brandy	1 teaspoon salt

First prepare the sauce in the following manner: In a heavy 2- to 3-quart saucepan, melt the 3 tablespoons of butter over moderate heat. When the foam begins to subside, add the onions and, stirring frequently, cook for about 5 minutes or until they are soft and translucent but not brown. Add the flour and mix well. Stirring constantly with a wire whisk, pour in the milk in a slow, thin stream and cook over high heat until the sauce comes to a boil, thickens and is smooth. Reduce the heat to low and simmer uncovered for 2 or 3 minutes to remove any taste of raw flour.

In a small pan, warm the brandy over low heat and ignite it with a match, then slide the pan back and forth gently until the flames die. Stir the brandy, the lemon juice, ⅛ teaspoon of ground red pepper and 1 teaspoon of salt into the sauce and taste for seasoning. Remove the pan from the heat and cover to keep the sauce warm until you are ready to use it.

CRABMEAT AND EGGS
8 tablespoons butter, cut into
 ½-inch bits
1 pound fresh, frozen or canned
 crabmeat, thoroughly drained and
 picked over to remove all bits of
shell and cartilage
⅛ teaspoon ground hot red pepper
 (cayenne)
½ teaspoon salt
8 very fresh eggs
½ teaspoon paprika

Preheat the oven to 450°. In a heavy 12-inch skillet, melt 6 tablespoons of the butter bits over moderate heat. Add the crabmeat and toss gently about with a spoon until the meat is hot and evenly moistened. Stir in ⅛ teaspoon of red pepper and ½ teaspoon of salt and, with a rubber spatula, scrape the contents of the skillet into an 8- to 10-inch round shallow baking-serving dish. Drape with foil to keep the crabmeat warm.

To poach the eggs, pour cold water into a 12-inch skillet to a depth of about 2 inches. Bring to a simmer, then reduce the heat so that the surface of the liquid barely shimmers. Break the eggs into individual saucers. Gently slide one egg into the water and, with a large spoon, lift the white over the yolk. Repeat once or twice more to enclose the yolk in the white.

One at a time, slide the seven other eggs into the pan, enclosing them in their whites and spacing them an inch apart. Poach the eggs for 3 or 4 minutes, until the whites are set and the yolks feel soft to the touch.

With a slotted spatula, arrange the poached eggs on the crabmeat. Spoon the brandied cream sauce over the eggs and sprinkle the top with the remaining 2 tablespoons of butter bits and the paprika. Bake in the middle of the oven for 10 minutes, or until the top is golden brown. Serve the eggs Nouvelle Orléans at once, directly from the baking dish.

Creamed Egg Chartres

To serve 8

1 tablespoon butter, softened, plus
   8 tablespoons butter, cut into
   ½-inch bits
5 medium-sized onions, peeled and
   cut crosswise into ⅛-inch-thick
   rounds
¾ cup flour
3 egg yolks, plus 12 hard-cooked

eggs, cut crosswise into ¼-inch-
   thick slices
6 cups milk
1½ teaspoons salt
1 teaspoon ground hot red pepper
   (cayenne)
1 cup freshly grated imported
   Parmesan cheese
3 tablespoons paprika

Preheat the oven to 350°. With a pastry brush, spread the tablespoon of softened butter evenly over the bottom and sides of a 14-by-9-by-2-inch baking-serving dish. Set the dish aside.

In a heavy 12-inch skillet, melt the 8 tablespoons of butter bits over moderate heat. When the foam begins to subside, add the onions and, stirring frequently, cook for about 8 minutes, or until they are soft and translucent but not brown. Add the flour and mix well, then reduce the heat to low and simmer for 3 or 4 minutes to remove the raw taste of the flour.

Meanwhile, in a deep bowl, beat the egg yolks with a wire whisk or a rotary or electric beater until they are smooth. Beat in the milk, salt and red pepper, and set aside. Mix the Parmesan cheese and paprika together in a bowl and reserve them.

Stirring the onion mixture constantly with a wire whisk, pour in the egg yolks and milk in a slow, thin stream and cook over high heat until the sauce comes to a boil, thickens heavily and is smooth. Taste the sauce for seasoning, remove the skillet from the heat and gently stir in nine of the sliced hard-cooked eggs.

Pour the eggs and sauce into the buttered dish and scatter the Parmesan cheese mixture evenly over the top. Bake in the middle of the oven for about 15 minutes, or until the top is browned and the sauce begins to bubble. Garnish the top with the remaining hard-cooked egg slices and serve at once, directly from the baking dish.

SHELLFISH

Shellfish Boil

In Louisiana, a "boil" is a mixture of dried spices used to flavor the stock in which crawfish, shrimp or blue crabs are boiled.

To make about 1 cup

¼ cup mustard seeds
¼ cup coriander seeds
2 tablespoons dill seeds
2 tablespoons whole allspice
1 tablespoon ground cloves
4 dried hot red chilies, each about
    1½ inches long, washed,
    stemmed and coarsely crumbled
    (caution: see note, page 6)
3 medium-sized bay leaves, finely
    crumbled

Mix the mustard, coriander, dill, allspice, cloves, chilies and bay leaves together in a jar, cover tightly and store the boil at room temperature.

Boiled Crawfish

To serve 4 to 6

6 to 8 quarts water
2 lemons, cut in half crosswise
4 medium-sized onions, with skins
   intact
2 celery stalks, including the leaves,
   cut into 3-inch lengths
1 dried hot red chili *(caution: see
   note, page 6)*

4 garlic cloves, peeled and bruised
   with the flat of a cleaver or large
   heavy knife
1 cup shellfish boil *(page 43)*, or
   substitute 1 cup commercial
   shrimp spice or crab boil
2 tablespoons salt
20 pounds live crawfish

Combine the water, lemons, onions, celery, chili, garlic, shellfish boil and salt in a 10- to 12-quart enameled pot, and bring to a boil over high heat. Cover tightly, reduce the heat to low, and cook for 20 minutes.

Meanwhile, soak the live crawfish in a sinkful of cold water for at least 10 minutes, then wash them thoroughly—a small batch at a time —in a colander set under cold running water.

With tongs, drop about 5 pounds of the live crawfish into the pot and boil briskly, uncovered, for 5 minutes. Transfer the boiled crawfish to a heated platter, then drop about 5 more pounds of live crawfish into the stock remaining in the pot and boil them for 5 minutes. Repeat the entire procedure two more times and, when all of the crawfish have been boiled, serve them at once in their shells (directions on how to crack and eat crawfish, opposite). Because they are so highly spiced, they are eaten without any accompaniment except cold beer.

NOTE: In Louisiana, crabs and shrimp are boiled and served in the same fashion as crawfish. Substitute three dozen live blue crabs or 4 pounds of large shrimp in their shells for the crawfish, and boil them in one batch. Boil the crabs for 10 to 15 minutes, the shrimp 5 minutes.

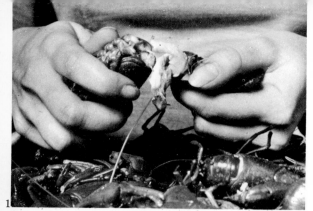

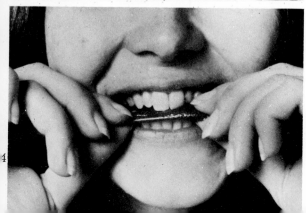

Eating boiled crawfish is a
basic skill in Louisiana
—but one that outsiders
can easily master.
(1) Holding the crawfish in
both hands, snap off the
ridged tail. In most cases,
the yellow fat can then be
pulled out of the head
shell, as shown here.
(2) With your thumbs, break
the tail shell in half
lengthwise. (3) Then pull
the meat out of the tail.
This is the most edible part
of the crawfish, though any
yellow fat left in the head
shell, scooped out with the
tip of a finger, is also
delicious. (4) Before
discarding the shells, you
may want to crack the
larger claws with your
teeth and suck out the
delicate claw meat.

Crawfish Pie

To make one 9-inch pie

PASTRY DOUGH
4 cups sifted all-purpose flour
½ teaspoon salt
½ pound unsalted butter, chilled
and cut into ¼-inch bits
½ pound lard, chilled and cut into
¼-inch bits
8 to 12 tablespoons ice water

First prepare the pastry dough in the following manner: Combine the 4 cups of sifted flour and ½ teaspoon of salt, and sift them together into a large chilled mixing bowl. Drop in the ½ pound of butter bits and the lard and, working quickly, use your fingertips to rub the flour and fat together until the mixture looks like flakes of coarse meal. Pour 8 tablespoons of ice water over the mixture all at once, and gather the dough into a ball.

If the dough crumbles, add up to 4 tablespoons more ice water, 1 teaspoon at a time, until the particles adhere. Dust lightly with flour, wrap the dough in wax paper and chill for 30 minutes.

Place the dough on a lightly floured board or table, and press it into a rectangular shape about 1 inch thick. Dust a little flour over and under it, and roll it out into a strip about 21 inches long and 12 inches wide. Fold the strip into thirds to form a three-layered rectangular packet, reducing its dimensions to about 7 by 12 inches.

Turn the dough around so that an open end faces you and roll it out once more to a 21-by-12-inch strip. Fold it into thirds as before and roll it out again to a similar strip. Repeat this entire process twice more, ending with the dough folded into a 7-by-12-inch packet.

Wrap the dough tightly in wax paper, foil or a plastic bag, and refrigerate it for at least 1 hour. The dough may be kept in the refrigerator for 3 or 4 days before it is used.

FILLING
10 pounds live crawfish
4 tablespoons butter
2 cups finely chopped onions
1 cup finely chopped scallions,
    including 3 inches of the green
    tops
½ cup finely chopped celery
½ cup finely chopped green pepper
1½ teaspoons finely chopped
    garlic
¼ cup unsifted flour
1 tablespoon canned tomato paste
½ cup finely chopped fresh
    parsley, preferably the flat-leaf
    Italian variety
½ teaspoon ground hot red pepper
    (cayenne)
½ teaspoon salt

1 tablespoon butter, softened

To make the pie filling, soak the live crawfish in cold water for at least 10 minutes, then wash them thoroughly, a small batch at a time, in a sieve or colander set under cold running water. In a heavy 8- to 10-quart pot, bring about 4 quarts of water to a boil over high heat. Using tongs, drop in the crawfish and boil them briskly, uncovered, for 5 minutes.

Drain the crawfish and, when they are cool enough to handle, shell them one at a time in the following manner: With your hands, break off the ridged tail, snap it in half lengthwise and lift out the meat in one piece. If you like, you can snap off the large claws, break them with a nut-cracker and pick out the bits of claw meat. (There should be about 4 cups of crawfish meat.)

Some or all of the yellow fat, or "butter," from the body of the craw-fish may slide out when you break off the tail. If it does not, cut off the top of the shell just behind the eyes, scoop the shell clean with the tip of a finger or your thumb and pick out the yellow fat. Place the crawfish meat and fat in a deep bowl and set it aside.

In a heavy 10- to 12-inch skillet, melt the 4 tablespoons of butter over moderate heat. Add the onions, scallions, celery, green pepper and garlic and, stirring frequently, cook for about 5 minutes, or until they are soft and translucent but not brown.

Remove the skillet from the heat and stir in the ¼ cup of unsifted flour. When it is well incorporated, add the tomato paste, parsley, red pepper and ½ teaspoon of salt. With a rubber spatula, scrape the entire contents of the skillet over the crawfish meat and fat and toss them together gently but thoroughly.

Preheat the oven to 350°. To assemble the pie, spread the tablespoon of softened butter over the bottom and sides of a 9-inch pie pan. Cut off half the chilled dough and, on a lightly floured surface, pat it into a circle about 1 inch thick. Dust a little flour over and under it and roll it out from the center to within an inch of the far edge of the dough. Lift the dough and turn it clockwise about 2 inches; roll again from the center to within an inch or so of the far edge. Repeat—lifting, turning, rolling —until the circle is about ¼ inch thick and 13 to 14 inches in diameter.

Drape the dough over the rolling pin, lift it up and unroll it over the buttered pie pan. Gently press the dough into the bottom and sides of the pan, being careful not to stretch it. With scissors cut the excess dough from the edges leaving a 1-inch overhang around the outside rim. Fill the pie shell with the crawfish mixture, mounding it somewhat higher in the center. Then roll out the remaining half of the dough into a 13-inch circle about ¼ inch thick.

With a pastry brush dipped in cold water, lightly moisten the outside edge of the pastry shell. Drape the circle of dough over the rolling pin, lift it up and drape it gently over the filling.

With scissors cut off the pastry even with the bottom crust, then crimp the top and bottom crusts together firmly with your fingers or press them together with the tines of a fork. Trim the excess pastry from around the rim with a sharp knife and cut two or three 1-inch-long parallel slits about ½ inch apart in the top of the pie.

Bake in the middle of the oven for 45 minutes, or until the crust is golden brown. Serve the crawfish pie at once.

Crawfish Étouffée

Étouffée literally means "smothered," and in this dish the crawfish tails are blanketed with a rich, thick sauce.

To serve 4

5 pounds live crawfish
2 cups freshly made fish stock
   (page 6)
4 tablespoons brown *roux (page 3)*
1 cup finely chopped onions
1 cup finely chopped scallions,
   including 3 inches of the green
   tops
½ cup finely chopped celery
1 teaspoon finely chopped garlic

A 1-pound can tomatoes, drained
   and finely chopped
1 tablespoon Worcestershire sauce
¼ teaspoon ground hot red pepper
   (cayenne)
1 teaspoon freshly ground black
   pepper
2 teaspoons salt
4 to 6 cups freshly cooked long-
   grain white rice

Soak the live crawfish in cold water for at least 10 minutes, then wash them thoroughly under cold running water. In a heavy 8- to 10-quart pot, bring 4 quarts of water to a boil over high heat. Using tongs, drop in the crawfish and boil them briskly, uncovered, for 5 minutes.

Drain the crawfish into a large colander and, when they are cool enough to handle, shell them one at a time in the following manner: With your hands, break off the ridged tail, snap it in half lengthwise and lift out the meat in one piece. If you like, you can snap off the large claws, break them with a nutcracker and pick out the bits of claw meat.

Some or all of the yellow fat or "butter" from the body of the crawfish may slide out when you break off the tail. If it does not, scoop the shell clean with the tip of one thumb and pick out the yellow fat. Reserve the crawfish meat and fat (there will be about 2 cups). Discard the shells, heads and intestinal matter.

Bring the fish stock to a boil in a small saucepan set over high heat. Remove the pan from the heat and cover to keep the stock hot.

In a heavy 5- to 6-quart casserole, warm the brown *roux* over low heat for 2 or 3 minutes, stirring constantly with a spoon. Add the onions, scallions, celery and garlic and, stirring frequently, cook over moderate heat for about 5 minutes, or until the vegetables are soft. Then, stirring constantly, pour in the hot fish stock in a slow, thin stream and cook over high heat until the mixture comes to a boil and thickens lightly.

Add the tomatoes, Worcestershire, red pepper, black pepper and salt, and reduce the heat to low. Simmer partially covered for 30 minutes, then stir in the crawfish meat and fat and heat them through.

Taste for seasoning and ladle the crawfish *étouffée* into a heated bowl. Mound the rice in a separate bowl and serve at once.

Crawfish Jambalaya

To serve 4

5 pounds live crawfish
¼ cup vegetable oil
½ cup finely chopped onions
½ cup finely chopped scallions, including 3 inches of the green tops
½ cup finely chopped celery
½ cup finely chopped green pepper
1 teaspoon finely chopped garlic

1 cup uncooked white rice, preferably broken rice (see Glossary, page 150)
¼ teaspoon ground hot red pepper (cayenne)
2½ teaspoons salt
2 cups water
¼ cup finely chopped fresh parsley, preferably the flat-leaf Italian variety

Soak the live crawfish in cold water for at least 10 minutes, then wash them thoroughly under cold running water. In a heavy 8- to 10-quart pot, bring about 4 quarts of water to a boil over high heat. Using tongs, drop in the crawfish and boil them briskly, uncovered, for 5 minutes.

Drain the crawfish into a colander and, when they are cool enough to handle, shell them one at a time in the following manner: With your hands, break off the ridged tail, snap it in half lengthwise and lift out the meat in one piece. If you like, you can snap off the large claws, break them with a nutcracker and pick out the bits of claw meat.

Some or all of the yellow fat, or "butter," from the body of the crawfish may slide out when you break off the tail. If it does not, scoop the body shell clean with the tip of a finger or your thumb and pick out the fat. Reserve the crawfish meat and fat (there will be about 2 cups). Discard the shells, heads and intestinal matter.

In a heavy 3-quart casserole, heat the oil over moderate heat until a light haze forms above it. Add the onions, scallions, celery, green pepper and garlic and, stirring frequently, cook for about 5 minutes, or until the vegetables are soft but not brown.

Stir in the rice and, when the grains are coated with oil, add the reserved crawfish meat and fat, the red pepper and salt. Stirring constantly, pour in the 2 cups of water in a slow, thin stream and bring to a boil over high heat. Reduce the heat to low, cover the casserole tightly and simmer for 25 minutes, or until all the liquid has been absorbed by the rice and the grains are tender but not too soft.

Add the chopped parsley and mix well, then taste for seasoning. Serve the crawfish jambalaya at once, directly from the casserole or mounded attractively in a large heated bowl.

Shrimp-and-Ham Jambalaya

To serve 6 to 8

2 cups water

2 teaspoons salt

1 cup broken white rice *(see Glossary, page 150)* or 1 cup short-grain white rice

2 pounds uncooked medium-sized shrimp (about 20 to 24 to the pound)

6 tablespoons butter

1½ cups finely chopped onions

2 tablespoons finely chopped garlic

A 1-pound can tomatoes, drained and finely chopped, with all their liquid

3 tablespoons canned tomato paste

½ cup finely chopped celery

¼ cup finely chopped green pepper

1 tablespoon finely chopped fresh parsley, preferably the flat-leaf Italian variety

3 whole cloves, pulverized with a mortar and pestle or finely crushed with a kitchen mallet or the flat of a heavy cleaver

½ teaspoon crumbled dried thyme

½ teaspoon ground hot red pepper (cayenne)

¼ teaspoon freshly ground black pepper

1 pound cooked lean smoked ham, trimmed of excess fat and cut into ½-inch cubes

Bring the water and 1 teaspoon of the salt to a boil in a small saucepan set over high heat. Add the rice, stir once or twice, and immediately cover the pan. Reduce the heat to low and simmer for about 20 minutes, or until the rice is tender and the grains have absorbed all of the liquid in the pan. Fluff the rice with a fork, cover, and set it aside.

Meanwhile, shell the shrimp. Devein them by making a shallow incision down their backs with a small sharp knife and lifting out the black or white intestinal vein with the point of the knife. Wash the shrimp briefly in a colander set under cold running water. Drop the shrimp into enough boiling salted water to cover them completely and cook briskly, uncovered, for 4 to 5 minutes, or until they are pink and firm. With a slotted spoon, transfer the shrimp to a bowl and set aside.

In a heavy 5- to 6-quart casserole, melt the butter over moderate heat. When the foam begins to subside, add the onions and garlic and, stirring frequently, cook for about 5 minutes, or until they are soft and translucent but not brown. Add the tomatoes, the tomato liquid and the tomato paste, and stir over moderate heat for 5 minutes. Then add the celery, green pepper, parsley, cloves, thyme, red pepper, black pepper and the remaining teaspoon of salt. Stirring frequently, cook uncovered over moderate heat until the vegetables are tender and the mixture is thick enough to hold its shape lightly in the spoon.

Add the ham and, stirring frequently, cook for 5 minutes. Then stir in the shrimp and, when they are heated through, add the reserved rice. Stir over moderate heat until the mixture is hot and the rice has absorbed any liquid in the pan.

Taste for seasoning and serve the shrimp-and-ham jambalaya at once, directly from the casserole or mounded in a heated bowl.

Shrimp Creole

To serve 6

12 medium-sized firm ripe tomatoes or 4 cups coarsely chopped drained canned tomatoes	2 teaspoons finely chopped garlic
	1 cup water
	2 medium-sized bay leaves
3 pounds uncooked medium-sized shrimp (about 20 to 24 to the pound)	1 tablespoon paprika
	½ teaspoon ground hot red pepper (cayenne)
½ cup vegetable oil	1 tablespoon salt
2 cups coarsely chopped onions	2 tablespoons cornstarch mixed with ¼ cup cold water
1 cup coarsely chopped green peppers	6 to 8 cups freshly cooked long-grain white rice
1 cup coarsely chopped celery	

If you are using fresh tomatoes, drop them three or four at a time into a pan of boiling water and remove them after 15 seconds. Run cold water over them and peel them with a small sharp knife. Cut out the stems, then slice the tomatoes in half crosswise, and squeeze the halves gently to remove the seeds and juice. Chop the tomatoes coarsely. (Canned tomatoes need only be thoroughly drained and chopped.)

Shell the shrimp. Devein them by making a shallow incision down the back with a small sharp knife and lifting out the black or white intestinal vein with the point of the knife. Wash the shrimp in a colander set under cold running water and spread them on paper towels to drain.

In a heavy 4- to 5-quart casserole, heat the oil over moderate heat until a light haze forms above it. Add the onions, green peppers, celery and garlic and, stirring frequently, cook for about 5 minutes, or until the vegetables are soft and translucent but not brown.

Stir in the tomatoes, water, bay leaves, paprika, red pepper and salt, and bring to a boil over high heat. Reduce the heat to low, cover the casserole partially and, stirring occasionally, simmer the mixture for 20 to 25 minutes, or until it is thick enough to hold its shape almost solidly in a spoon. Stir in the shrimp and continue to simmer, partially covered, for about 5 minutes longer, or until they are pink and firm to the touch.

Stir the cornstarch-and-water mixture once or twice to recombine it, and pour it into the casserole. Stir over low heat for 2 or 3 minutes, until the sauce thickens slightly. Pick out and discard the bay leaves, then taste the sauce for seasoning.

Serve the shrimp Creole at once, directly from the casserole, accompanied by the rice in a separate bowl. Or, if you prefer, mound the rice on a deep heated platter and ladle the shrimp Creole around it.

Stuffed Shrimp

To serve 6

4 tablespoons butter
½ cup finely chopped onions
¼ cup finely chopped scallions, including 3 inches of the green tops
¼ cup finely chopped celery
¼ cup finely chopped green pepper
1 teaspoon finely chopped garlic
1 pound fresh, frozen or canned crabmeat, thoroughly drained, picked over to remove all bits of shell and cartilage, and torn into small shreds
1 tablespoon finely chopped fresh parsley, preferably the flat-leaf Italian variety
¼ teaspoon ground hot red pepper (cayenne)
1½ teaspoons salt
24 uncooked jumbo shrimp (about 2 pounds)
2 eggs
½ cup evaporated milk
1 cup flour
2 cups soft fresh crumbs made from French- or Italian-type white bread, pulverized in a blender
Vegetable oil for deep frying
1 lemon, cut lengthwise into 6 wedges

In a heavy 10- to 12-inch skillet, melt the butter over moderate heat. When the foam begins to subside, add the onions, scallions, celery, green pepper and garlic and, stirring frequently, cook for about 5 minutes, or until the vegetables are soft but not brown. Stir in the crabmeat, parsley, red pepper and ½ teaspoon of the salt, and remove the pan from the heat. Taste the stuffing mixture for seasoning.

Shell the shrimp, leaving the last section of shell and the tail intact. Devein them by making a shallow incision down their backs with a small sharp knife and lifting out the black or white intestinal vein with the point of the knife. Wash the shrimp briefly in a colander set under cold running water, spread them on paper towels to drain and pat them completely dry with fresh paper towels.

Butterfly the shrimp by cutting along their outer curves about three quarters of the way through and carefully flattening them with the palm of your hand. Sprinkle the shrimp with the remaining teaspoon of salt and spoon the stuffing mixture in a band down the center of each shrimp, dividing it equally among them. Fold the long edges of the shrimp back together, and hold them in place with toothpicks if necessary.

Combine the eggs and evaporated milk in a shallow bowl and beat them with a wire whisk or a fork until the mixture is smooth. Spread the flour and the bread crumbs on separate plates or pieces of wax paper. One at a time, roll the shrimp in the flour to coat them evenly, immerse them in the beaten-egg mixture, and turn them about in the bread crumbs. As you proceed, arrange the breaded shrimp side by side on a baking sheet lined with wax paper. Refrigerate the shrimp for about 1 hour to firm their coating.

Preheat the oven to its lowest setting. At the same time, line a large shallow baking dish with a double thickness of paper towels and place it on the middle shelf of the oven. If you have used toothpicks to secure the shrimp, remove them.

Pour vegetable oil into a deep fryer or large heavy saucepan to a depth of 2 or 3 inches and heat the oil until it reaches a temperature of 375° on a deep-frying thermometer.

Deep-fry the shrimp, three or four at a time, turning them gently with a slotted spoon for 4 to 5 minutes, or until they crisp and brown on all sides. As they brown, transfer them to the paper-lined dish and keep them warm in the oven while you deep-fry the rest.

Arrange the shrimp attractively on a deep platter, garnish with the lemon wedges and serve at once.

Oyster Pie

To make one 9-inch pie

1½ cups unsifted flour
1½ teaspoons double-acting baking powder
½ teaspoon salt
2 tablespoons butter, chilled and cut into ½-inch bits plus 1 tablespoon butter, softened
¾ cup sour cream
4 slices lean bacon
¼ cup finely chopped onions

½ cup finely chopped scallions, including 3 inches of the green tops
¼ cup finely chopped fresh parsley, preferably the flat-leaf Italian variety
½ teaspoon ground hot red pepper (cayenne)
1 quart shucked oysters, thoroughly drained

First prepare the pastry dough in the following manner: Combine the flour, baking powder and salt, and sift them into a deep bowl. Add the 2 tablespoons of butter bits and, with your fingers, rub the flour and fat together until they resemble flakes of coarse meal. Add the sour cream and beat vigorously with a wooden spoon until the dough is smooth and can be gathered into a compact ball. Wrap the ball in wax paper and refrigerate the dough while you prepare the oyster filling.

In a heavy 8-inch skillet, fry the bacon over moderate heat, turning it frequently with tongs until it is crisp and brown and has rendered all its fat. Transfer the bacon to paper towels to drain and, when it is cool, crumble it into small bits.

Add the onions to the fat remaining in the skillet and, stirring frequently, cook for about 5 minutes, or until they are soft and translucent but not brown. With a rubber spatula, scrape the entire contents of the skillet into a bowl. Add the reserved bacon bits, the scallions, parsley and red pepper, and mix well. Drop in the oysters and turn them about with a spoon to coat them evenly.

Continued on next page

Preheat the oven to 375°. With a pastry brush, spread the tablespoon of softened butter over the bottom and sides of a 9-inch ovenproof glass pie plate. Place the oyster filling in the buttered pie plate.

Place the chilled dough on a lightly floured surface and pat it into a circle about 1 inch thick. Dust a little flour over and under it and roll it out from the center to within an inch of the far edge of the dough. Lift the dough and turn it clockwise about 2 inches; roll again from the center to within an inch or so of the far edge. Repeat—lifting, turning, rolling —until the circle is about ⅓ inch thick and 9 inches in diameter.

Drape the dough over the rolling pin, lift it up and unroll it over the pie. With a sharp knife, cut the excess dough from around the edges so that the pastry fits snugly into the pie plate. Score the dough with criss-crossing diagonal lines about 1½ inches apart to create a diamond pattern on the surface of the pie.

Bake in the middle of the oven for 25 to 30 minutes, or until the dough is puffed and delicately browned and the filling is bubbly. At the table, use a pie server to cut the oyster pie into wedges and turn each portion upside down on a plate with the crust beneath the filling.

Peacemaker

OYSTER LOAF SANDWICH

To serve 2

1 pint medium-sized shucked oysters (about 12 oysters)
¼ teaspoon ground hot red pepper (cayenne)
¼ teaspoon freshly ground black pepper
2 eggs
½ cup evaporated milk
⅛ teaspoon salt
1 cup unsifted corn flour (see Glossary, page 150) or 1 cup all-purpose flour
1½ cups soft fresh crumbs made from French- or Italian-type white bread, pulverized in a blender
1 loaf French- or Italian-type bread about 15 inches long and 3 inches wide
4 tablespoons butter, melted
Vegetable oil for deep frying
½ cup Creole tartar sauce (page 60)
1½ cups finely shredded lettuce
1 large tomato, washed, stemmed and cut crosswise into ¼-inch-thick slices

In the 19th Century, according to tradition, a New Orleans husband who had spent the night in the French Quarter saloons brought this oyster loaf sandwich home to his wife as a médiatrice, or peacemaker. Called a "poor boy" in New Orleans, this kind of sandwich is known in other sections of the United States as a hero, a grinder or a submarine.

Pat the oysters completely dry with paper towels and season them on all sides with the red and black pepper. In a shallow bowl, beat the eggs to a froth with a wire whisk or fork, add the evaporated milk and salt, and mix well. Spread the corn flour or all-purpose flour on one piece of wax paper and the bread crumbs on another piece.

Roll one oyster at a time in the flour and, when it is evenly covered, immerse it in the egg mixture. Then turn the oyster about in the crumbs to coat it on all sides. Arrange the oysters in one layer on a plate and refrigerate them while you prepare the bread.

Preheat the oven to 350°. With a large sharp knife, slice the loaf of bread horizontally in half. Pull out all the white doughy crumbs from both the top and bottom to create two boatlike shells of the crusts. With a pastry brush, spread the melted butter evenly inside both halves of the loaf. Place the shells on a baking sheet and bake in the middle of the oven for about 15 minutes, or until they are crisp and lightly brown.

Meanwhile, pour vegetable oil into a deep fryer or large heavy saucepan to a depth of about 3 inches and heat the oil until it reaches a temperature of 375°. Deep-fry the oysters, six at a time, turning them with a slotted spoon for 2 to 3 minutes, or until the coating is crisp and golden brown. As they brown, transfer them to paper towels to drain.

To assemble the peacemaker, spread the tartar sauce inside both the bottom and top parts of the loaf. Scatter the shredded lettuce on the bottom half of the loaf and arrange the tomato slices and finally the oysters over it. Set the top part of the loaf in place, slice the loaf crosswise into four portions and serve at once.

NOTE: If you prefer, you may omit the sliced tomatoes from the sandwich and instead of using the Creole tartar sauce spread the inside top and bottom of the loaf with a mixture of ½ cup of bottled chili sauce, 2 tablespoons of prepared horseradish, 2 teaspoons of strained fresh lemon juice and ¼ teaspoon of Worcestershire sauce.

Crab Chops

To serve 6

10 tablespoons butter
¼ cup flour
1 cup milk
½ teaspoon ground hot red pepper (cayenne)
1 teaspoon salt
1 pound (about 3 cups) fresh, frozen or canned crabmeat, thoroughly drained and picked over to remove all bits of shell and cartilage
¼ cup finely chopped fresh parsley plus fresh parsley sprigs for garnish, both preferably the flat-leaf Italian variety
¼ cup finely chopped scallions, including 3 inches of the green tops
3 eggs
3 cups soft fresh crumbs made from French- or Italian-type bread, pulverized in a blender
2 tablespoons vegetable oil
6 cooked blue-crab claws, in their shells (optional)
1 lemon, cut lengthwise into 6 wedges
Creole tartar sauce *(page 60)*

In a heavy 1- to 1½-quart saucepan, melt 4 tablespoons of the butter over moderate heat. Add the flour and mix well. Stirring constantly with a wire whisk, pour in the milk in a slow, thin stream and cook over high heat until the mixture comes to a boil, thickens heavily and is smooth. Reduce the heat to low and simmer uncovered for 2 or 3 minutes.

Stir in the red pepper and salt and, with a rubber spatula, scrape the entire contents of the pan into a deep bowl. Add the crabmeat, chopped parsley and scallions, and mix all the ingredients gently but thoroughly. Taste for seasoning. Cover the bowl with foil or plastic wrap and refrigerate for at least 2 hours, or until the crab mixture is somewhat firm.

Break the eggs into a shallow bowl and beat them to a froth with a fork or wire whisk. Spread the bread crumbs on a platter or a piece of wax paper. Divide the crab mixture into six equal portions and, with your hand, pat each portion into a teardrop-shaped "chop" about 5 inches long and ½ inch thick. As you form each chop, place it in the bread crumbs and turn it carefully to coat both sides. Immerse the chop in the beaten eggs and then turn it over in the crumbs again to bread it evenly. As you proceed, arrange the crab chops side by side in a large pan lined with wax paper. Refrigerate them for at least 30 minutes to firm the coating.

In a heavy 12-inch skillet, melt the remaining 6 tablespoons of butter with the oil over moderate heat. When the foam begins to subside, add the crab chops and, turning them once with a metal spatula, fry them for about 10 minutes, or until they are delicately browned on both sides.

Arrange the crab chops on a heated platter or individual plates and, if you wish, insert a crab claw at the narrow end of each chop. Garnish with the lemon wedges and parsley sprigs, and serve the crab chops at once, accompanied by a bowl of Creole tartar sauce.

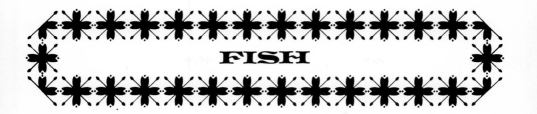

Speckled Trout Amandine

To serve 6

Vegetable oil for deep frying
2 eggs
1 cup unsifted flour
6 four-ounce speckled trout or
   weakfish fillets, skinned
1 teaspoon salt
¼ teaspoon ground white pepper
½ pound butter, cut into ½-inch

bits
1 cup finely chopped blanched
   almonds
¼ cup strained fresh lemon juice
2 tablespoons finely chopped fresh
   parsley, preferably the flat-leaf
   Italian variety
1 teaspoon Worcestershire sauce

Preheat the oven to its lowest setting. At the same time, line a large shallow baking dish with a double thickness of paper towels and place it on the middle shelf of the oven.

Pour vegetable oil into a deep fryer or large heavy saucepan to a depth of 2 to 3 inches and heat the oil until it reaches a temperature of 360° on a deep-frying thermometer.

Meanwhile, break the eggs into a shallow bowl and beat them to a froth with a fork or wire whisk. Spread the flour out on wax paper.

Pat the fish fillets completely dry with paper towels and season them with the salt and white pepper. Roll one fillet at a time in the flour, immerse it in the beaten eggs, then roll it in the flour again to coat it evenly. Shake the fillet to remove the excess flour and set it aside on a plate.

Deep-fry the fillets, two or three at a time, for about 6 minutes, or until they are crisp and golden on both sides. As they brown, transfer the fillets to the paper-lined pan and keep them warm in the oven while you deep-fry the rest.

When all the fillets are cooked, prepare the sauce in the following manner: In a heavy 10- to 12-inch skillet, melt the butter bits over moderate heat, stirring frequently so that the butter melts completely without burning. As soon as the butter begins to brown, add the almonds and toss them about with a spoon to moisten them evenly. Stir in the lemon juice, parsley and Worcestershire sauce, and taste the sauce for seasoning.

To serve, arrange the fillets attractively on a heated platter or individual serving plates and pour the sauce over them.

Speckled Trout Marguery

To serve 4

2 tablespoons butter, softened, plus 2 tablespoons butter, cut into ½-inch bits

¼ pound firm fresh mushrooms, trimmed, wiped with a dampened towel and cut lengthwise, including the stems, into ¼-inch-thick slices

¼ cup thinly sliced scallions, including 3 inches of the green tops

4 eight-ounce speckled trout or weakfish fillets, skinned

1½ teaspoons salt

½ cup dry white wine

12 medium-sized uncooked shrimp (about ½ pound)

1 cup hollandaise sauce *(page 5)*

2 tablespoons coarsely chopped black truffles

⅛ teaspoon ground hot red pepper (cayenne)

Preheat the oven to 350°. With a pastry brush, spread 1 tablespoon of the softened butter on the bottom of a flameproof baking pan large enough to hold the fish fillets in one layer. Cut a piece of wax paper to fit snugly inside the pan and spread one side of the paper with the remaining tablespoon of softened butter.

Scatter the mushrooms and scallions over the bottom of the pan and lay the fish fillets over them, side by side. Sprinkle the tops with 1 teaspoon of the salt and pour in the wine. Bring to a simmer on top of the stove, cover the fish with the wax paper, buttered side down, and poach the fish in the middle of the oven for about 20 minutes, or until the fillets are firm to the touch.

Meanwhile, shell the shrimp. Devein them by making a shallow incision down their backs with a small sharp knife and lifting out the black or white intestinal vein with the point of the knife. Wash the shrimp briefly in a colander set under cold running water, spread them on paper towels to drain and pat them completely dry with fresh paper towels.

In a heavy 6- to 8-inch skillet, melt the 2 tablespoons of butter bits over moderate heat. When the foam begins to subside, add the shrimp and stir for 2 to 3 minutes, or until they are pink and firm to the touch. Set the skillet aside off the heat, and prepare the hollandaise sauce.

When the fillets have cooked the allotted time, use a slotted spatula to transfer them to an ovenproof platter. Strain the poaching liquid through a fine sieve into a small enameled saucepan and boil it over high heat until it has reduced to 2 tablespoons. With a wire whisk, beat the liquid into the hollandaise. Stir in the truffles, the red pepper and the remaining ½ teaspoon of salt, and taste the sauce for seasoning.

Preheat the broiler to its highest setting. To assemble the speckled trout Marguery, place three shrimp on each fillet and spoon the sauce over the top, masking the fish completely. Slide the platter under the broiler for 30 seconds, or until the sauce is lightly browned. Serve at once.

Frogs' Legs Sauce Piquante

To serve 4

2 dozen large individual frogs' legs (about 4 pounds), thoroughly defrosted if frozen
1 teaspoon ground hot red pepper (cayenne)
1½ teaspoons salt
½ cup vegetable oil
4 tablespoons brown *roux (page 3)*
½ cup finely chopped onions
2 tablespoons finely chopped green

pepper
2 tablespoons finely chopped celery
A 1-pound can tomatoes, drained and coarsely chopped, with all the liquid reserved
2 teaspoons finely chopped garlic
2 tablespoons finely chopped scallions
2 tablespoons finely chopped fresh parsley, preferably the flat-leaf Italian variety
1 lemon, thinly sliced

Pat the frogs' legs completely dry with paper towels and season them evenly on all sides with the red pepper and 1 teaspoon of the salt.

In a heavy 12-inch skillet (preferably one with a nonstick cooking surface) heat ¼ cup of the vegetable oil over moderate heat until a light haze forms above it. Add 12 of the frogs' legs and fry them for 4 or 5 minutes, turning them once or twice with tongs or a large metal spatula and regulating the heat so that they color richly and evenly without burning. As they are cooked, transfer the frogs' legs to a platter. Pour the remaining ¼ cup of vegetable oil into the skillet and, when it is hot, fry the other dozen frogs' legs in the same fashion.

Stirring constantly, add the brown *roux* to the fat remaining in the skillet. Drop in the onions, green pepper and celery and, stirring frequently, cook over moderate heat for about 5 minutes, or until the vegetables are soft. Stir in the tomatoes and their liquid, add the garlic and the remaining ½ teaspoon of salt and boil briskly, uncovered, for about 5 minutes longer. When the vegetable-sauce mixture is thick enough to hold its shape almost solidly in the spoon, return the frogs' legs and the liquid that has accumulated around them to the skillet.

Stirring and basting the frogs' legs with the sauce, cook for a minute or so longer to heat the legs through. Then mix in the scallions and parsley and taste for seasoning. (*Piquante* means "pungent," and the sauce should be distinctly peppery.)

With tongs or a slotted spoon, arrange the frogs' legs attractively on a large heated platter. Pour the *sauce piquante* over the frogs' legs, garnish the platter with the lemon slices, and serve at once.

NOTE: Louisiana cooks also use *sauce piquante* with turtle meat, shrimp, crawfish, fish and wild or domestic birds of every kind.

Fried Frogs' Legs

To serve 4

Vegetable oil for deep frying
2 dozen large individual frogs' legs
(about 4 pounds), thoroughly
defrosted if frozen
1 teaspoon ground hot red pepper
(cayenne)
2 teaspoons salt

1 cup yellow cornmeal
1 cup unsifted flour
4 eggs
¼ cup milk
2 lemons, each cut lengthwise into
4 or 6 wedges
Creole tartar sauce (below)

Preheat the oven to its lowest setting. Line a large shallow baking dish with paper towels and place it in the middle of the oven.

Pour vegetable oil into a deep fryer or large heavy saucepan to a depth of 2 to 3 inches and heat the oil until it reaches a temperature of 375° on a deep-frying thermometer.

Meanwhile, pat the frogs' legs completely dry with paper towels and season them on all sides with the red pepper and salt. Combine the cornmeal and flour in a shallow bowl and stir to mix well. Combine the eggs and milk in another shallow bowl and, with a fork or wire whisk, beat them together until the mixture is smooth.

Just before cooking, roll each frog's leg in the cornmeal mixture. Immerse it in the egg-and-milk mixture and then turn it about in the cornmeal mixture again to coat it evenly.

Deep-fry the frogs' legs in the hot oil, three or four at a time, turning them with a slotted spoon for about 5 minutes, or until they are golden brown and crisp on all sides. As they brown, transfer the frogs' legs to the lined dish and keep them warm in the oven while you cook the rest.

To serve the frogs' legs, mound them attractively on a heated platter and arrange the lemon wedges around the edge. Serve at once, accompanied by the Creole tartar sauce in a separate bowl.

Creole Tartar Sauce

To make about 2 to 3 cups

3 egg yolks
1½ cups olive oil
1 tablespoon Creole mustard (see
Glossary, page 150)
¼ teaspoon ground hot red pepper
(cayenne)
1½ teaspoons salt

½ cup finely chopped scallions,
including 3 inches of the green
tops
½ cup finely chopped fresh
parsley, preferably the flat-leaf
Italian variety
½ cup finely chopped dill pickles

With a wire whisk or a rotary or electric beater, beat the egg yolks vigorously in a deep bowl for about 2 minutes, until they thicken and cling to the whisk or beater when it is lifted from the bowl. Beat in ½ cup of the oil, ½ teaspoon at a time, making sure each addition is absorbed before adding more. By the time ½ cup of oil has been beaten in, the sauce should have the consistency of thick cream. Pour in the remaining oil in a slow, thin stream, beating constantly.

Add the Creole mustard, red pepper and salt, and continue to beat until the sauce is smooth. Then stir in the chopped scallions, parsley and pickles, and taste for seasoning.

The Creole tartar sauce may be served immediately. Or, if you prefer, it may be covered tightly and refrigerated for 2 or 3 days before serving.

Broiled Spanish Mackerel

To serve 4

4 tablespoons butter	½ teaspoon salt
1 tablespoon strained fresh lime juice	4 six-ounce Spanish mackerel fillets, skinned
½ teaspoon anchovy paste	1 tablespoon vegetable oil
⅛ teaspoon ground hot red pepper (cayenne)	1 lime, cut lengthwise into 4 or 8 wedges

Preheat the broiler to its highest setting. Melt the butter over moderate heat in a small saucepan. Remove the pan from the heat and stir in the lime juice, anchovy paste, red pepper and salt. Set the butter sauce aside.

Pat the mackerel fillets completely dry with paper towels. Then, with a pastry brush, spread the vegetable oil evenly over the grid of the broiling pan. Arrange the fillets side by side on the grid, and brush them with about 2 tablespoons of the butter sauce. Broil 4 inches from the heat for 4 to 5 minutes, brushing the fillets once or twice more with the remaining sauce. The mackerel is done when the tops are golden brown and the fish feel firm to the touch.

With a wide metal spatula, transfer the fillets to a heated platter. Arrange the lime wedges around the fish and serve at once.

Pompano en Papillote
POMPANO FILLETS WITH SHRIMP AND CRAB BAKED IN PARCHMENT PAPER

To serve 4

1 pound fish trimmings: the heads,
    tails and bones of any firm white
    fish
3 cups water
2 medium-sized onions, peeled and
    coarsely chopped
1 medium-sized bay leaf, crumbled
6 whole black peppercorns
2 teaspoons salt
3 tablespoons butter, softened, plus
    5 tablespoons butter, cut into
    small bits, plus 4 teaspoons
    butter, melted
4 eight-ounce pompano fillets, or
    substitute 4 eight-ounce sole or
    flounder fillets
½ cup dry white wine

½ pound uncooked small shrimp,
    preferably river shrimp (*see
    Glossary, page 150*)
¼ cup finely chopped scallions,
    including 3 inches of the green
    tops
2 tablespoons finely chopped fresh
    parsley, preferably the flat-leaf
    Italian variety
¼ cup flour
3 tablespoons heavy cream
¼ teaspoon ground hot red pepper
    (cayenne)
¼ pound freshly cooked, frozen or
    canned crabmeat, thoroughly
    drained and picked over to
    remove all bits of shell and
    cartilage

Combine the fish trimmings and water in a 3- to 4-quart enameled sauce-pan and bring to a boil over high heat, skimming off the foam and scum as they rise to the surface. Add the onions, bay leaf, peppercorns and salt, reduce the heat to low, and simmer, partially covered, for 30 minutes. Then strain the fish stock through a fine sieve set over a bowl, pressing the trimmings and seasonings with the back of a spoon to extract all their juices before discarding the bones and pulp. Set the stock aside.

Preheat the oven to 350°. With a pastry brush, spread 1 tablespoon of the softened butter evenly over the bottom and sides of a 13-by-9-by-2-inch baking dish. Cut a piece of wax paper to fit over the dish and brush one side of the paper with 1 tablespoon of softened butter.

Place the fish fillets in the buttered dish and pour the reserved stock and the wine over them. Cover the dish loosely with the buttered paper and bake in the middle of the oven for 5 minutes, or until the fillets feel firm when prodded gently with a finger. With a large metal spatula, transfer the fish to a platter. Measure the stock remaining in the baking dish and reserve 1½ cups. Increase the oven temperature to 450°.

Meanwhile, shell the shrimp. Unless you are using the river variety, devein the shrimp by making a shallow incision down their backs with a small sharp knife and lifting out the intestinal vein with the point of the knife. If the shrimp are over 1 inch long, cut them into pieces. Wash the shrimp briefly in a colander and pat them dry with paper towels.

Melt 2 tablespoons of the butter bits in a small skillet set over moderate heat. When the foam begins to subside, add the shrimp and stir for 2 to 3 minutes, until they are pink and firm to the touch. Set the shrimp aside off the heat.

Cut out four paper hearts about 11 inches long and 15 inches wide *(below)* and brush one side with melted butter. Set the hearts aside.

In a heavy 1- to 1½-quart saucepan, melt the remaining 3 table-spoons of butter bits over moderate heat. Add the scallions and parsley and, stirring frequently, cook for about 5 minutes, until they are soft but not brown. Add the flour and mix well. Then, stirring constantly with a wire whisk, pour in the reserved 1½ cups of stock in a slow, thin stream and cook over high heat until the sauce comes to a boil, thickens and is smooth. Reduce the heat to low and simmer the sauce uncovered for 3 minutes. Stir in the cream and red pepper, and taste for seasoning.

To assemble each pompano en papillote, place a fish fillet on one side of a paper heart and cover the fillet with about ¼ cup of shrimp and ¼ cup of crabmeat. Spoon the sauce over the top, dividing it equally among the four portions. Fold over the exposed side of the paper so that the edges of paper meet. Starting at the upper end of the fold, seal the edges by crimping them at about ½-inch intervals. Before crimping the bottom point of the heart, open the seam slightly and blow through the hole to inflate the papillote. Then quickly crimp the bottom point closed.

Brush a large baking sheet with the remaining tablespoon of softened butter and place the papillotes on it. Bake in the middle of the preheated 450° oven for 8 to 10 minutes. The paper should turn a golden brown. Serve the papillotes at once, opening the paper at the table.

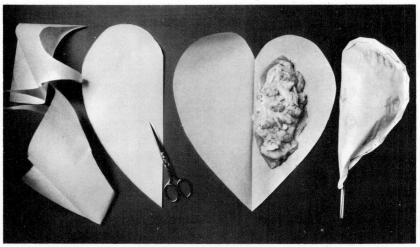

As its name indicates, pompano en papillote *(above)* is baked and served "in paper." For each serving, fold a large sheet of parchment paper in half as shown at left and use scissors to cut it into the shape of a heart about 11 inches long and 15 inches wide. Unfold the shape and lay it flat, then brush the surface evenly with softened butter. Place a fillet of fish on one side of the paper heart *(center)* and spoon the shrimp sauce over the fish. Then fold the heart over the sauced pompano and, starting at the upper end of the fold, seal the edges snugly together by crimping them at about ½-inch intervals *(right)*. Before crimping the bottom point of the heart, open the seam slightly and insert a drinking straw, as shown in the picture. Blow air through the straw to inflate the papillote, then quickly crimp the tip shut. Repeat the procedure until all of the pompano fillets are enclosed in their puffed paper hearts.

Shrimp-and-Crab-stuffed Flounder

To serve 4

1½ pounds uncooked shrimp

10 tablespoons butter, cut into ½-inch bits, plus 3 tablespoons butter, melted

1½ cups soft fresh crumbs made from French- or Italian-type white bread, pulverized in a blender

⅓ cup finely chopped onions

⅓ cup finely chopped green peppers

⅓ cup finely chopped celery

⅓ cup finely chopped scallions, including 3 inches of the green tops

2 teaspoons finely chopped garlic

⅓ cup finely chopped drained canned tomatoes

4 teaspoons Worcestershire sauce

1½ teaspoons Creole mustard *(see Glossary, page 150)*

½ teaspoon ground hot red pepper

2 teaspoons salt

1 pound (2 cups) fresh, frozen or canned crabmeat, thoroughly drained and picked over to remove all bits of shell or cartilage

3 tablespoons finely chopped fresh parsley, preferably the flat-leaf Italian variety

Four 1½-pound flounders, cleaned and with the heads removed but the tails intact

¼ teaspoon freshly ground black pepper

Shell the shrimp. Devein them by making a shallow incision down their backs with a small sharp knife and lifting out the black or white intestinal vein with the point of the knife. Wash the shrimp briefly in a colander set under cold running water.

Drop the shrimp into enough lightly salted boiling water to immerse them completely and boil briskly, uncovered, for 3 to 5 minutes, or until they are firm and pink. Drain the shrimp, spread them on paper towels, and pat them completely dry with fresh towels. Then chop the shrimp coarsely and reserve them.

In a heavy 10- to 12-inch skillet, melt 6 tablespoons of the butter bits over moderate heat. When the foam begins to subside, add the bread crumbs and stir until they are crisp and golden. With a rubber spatula, scrape the entire contents of the skillet into a deep bowl and set aside.

Add the remaining 4 tablespoons of butter bits to the skillet and melt them over moderate heat. Drop in the onions, green peppers, celery, scallions and garlic and, stirring frequently, cook for about 5 minutes, or until the vegetables are soft but not brown. Stir in the tomatoes, Worcestershire sauce, Creole mustard, red pepper and 1 teaspoon of the salt. Then scrape the mixture into the bowl with the bread crumbs. Add the reserved shrimp, the crabmeat and the parsley, and toss all the stuffing ingredients together gently but thoroughly. Taste for seasoning.

Preheat the oven to 400°. With a pastry brush, spread 1 tablespoon of the melted butter over the bottom and sides of a shallow baking-serving dish large enough to hold the flounders in one layer. Set aside.

Wash the fish under cold running water and pat them dry with paper towels. To prepare the flounders for stuffing, place one at a time on its belly (light-colored side) on the cutting board. With a small sharp knife, make a 4- to 5-inch-long slit completely through the skin and top surface of flesh to the backbone of the fish, cutting from about 1 inch behind the head to within about 1 inch of the tail.

With your fingers or the point of the knife, gently lift the top surface of the flesh away from the rows of small bones radiating from the backbone, to create pockets on both sides of the slit.

Sprinkle the remaining teaspoon of salt and the black pepper inside the pockets formed in the flounders. Then fill the pockets and the space between them with the shrimp-and-crab stuffing, dividing it equally among the four fish and mounding the stuffing in the centers.

Arrange the flounders side by side in the buttered dish and brush the tops with the remaining 2 tablespoons of melted butter. Bake on the middle shelf of the oven for about 20 minutes, or until the fish feel firm when prodded gently with a finger. Serve the shrimp-and-crab-stuffed flounder at once, directly from the baking dish.

Catfish Étouffée

To serve 4

2 cups freshly made fish stock (page 6)
4 tablespoons brown roux (page 3)
1 cup finely chopped onions
1 cup finely chopped scallions, including 3 inches of the green tops
½ cup finely chopped celery
½ cup finely chopped green pepper
1 teaspoon finely chopped garlic
A 1-pound can tomatoes, drained and coarsely chopped
Two ¼-inch-thick lemon slices

1 tablespoon Worcestershire sauce
1 small bay leaf, crumbled
¼ teaspoon crumbled dried thyme
¼ teaspoon ground hot red pepper (cayenne)
1 teaspoon freshly ground black pepper
2 teaspoons salt
2 pounds catfish fillets, skinned and cut into 1-inch chunks
½ cup finely chopped fresh parsley, preferably the flat-leaf Italian variety
4 cups freshly cooked white rice

The literal meaning of étouffée is "smothered," and in this dish the catfish is blanketed with a rich, thick sauce.

In a small saucepan, bring the fish stock to a boil over high heat. Remove the pan from the heat and cover to keep the stock hot.

Warm the brown roux in a heavy 4- to 5-quart casserole set over low heat, stirring all the while. Add the onions, scallions, celery, green pepper and garlic and, stirring frequently, cook for about 5 minutes, or until they are soft but not brown.

Continued on next page

Stirring constantly, pour in the hot fish stock in a slow, thin stream. Then add the tomatoes, lemon slices, Worcestershire sauce, bay leaf, thyme, red and black pepper and salt. Reduce the heat to low and simmer, partially covered, for 30 minutes.

Add the chunks of catfish and the parsley, and stir gently to moisten the fish evenly with the simmering sauce. Cover the casserole partially again and, without stirring, simmer for 10 minutes longer, or until the catfish flakes easily when prodded gently with a fork.

Taste for seasoning and serve the catfish *étouffée* at once, directly from the casserole or arranged attractively on a deep heated platter. Present the rice in a separate bowl.

Redfish Courtbouillon

To serve 6

6 tablespoons brown *roux (page 3)*	1 large bay leaf
½ cup finely chopped onions	½ teaspoon crumbled dried thyme
½ cup finely chopped celery	¼ teaspoon crumbled dried
½ cup finely chopped scallions	marjoram
2 teaspoons finely chopped garlic	¼ teaspoon ground allspice
3 cups coarsely chopped drained	2½ pounds redfish or red snapper
canned tomatoes	fillets, skinned and cut into
1 cup canned tomato purée	3-by-1-inch strips
1 cup finely chopped green peppers	2 tablespoons fresh lemon juice
1 cup fish stock *(page 6)*	½ teaspoon ground hot red pepper
½ cup dry red wine	(cayenne)

In a heavy 4- to 5-quart casserole, warm the brown *roux* over low heat for 2 or 3 minutes, stirring constantly. Add the onions, celery, scallions and garlic and, stirring occasionally, cook for about 5 minutes, or until the vegetables are soft.

Add the tomatoes, tomato purée, green peppers, fish stock, wine, bay leaf, thyme, marjoram and allspice and, stirring from time to time, cook briskly, uncovered, until the mixture is thick enough to hold its shape almost solidly in the spoon.

Drop in the strips of fish and turn them about with a spoon to coat them evenly. Stir in the lemon juice and red pepper, reduce the heat to low, and simmer tightly covered for 20 to 25 minutes, or until the fish flakes easily when prodded gently with a fork.

Remove and discard the bay leaf and taste the sauce for seasoning. Serve the redfish courtbouillon at once, directly from the casserole or from a heated serving bowl.

Broiled Redfish

To serve 6

4 tablespoons butter, cut into
½-inch bits, plus 2 tablespoons
butter, melted
½ cup finely chopped onions
1 teaspoon finely chopped garlic
½ cup fish stock *(page 6)*
¼ cup finely chopped green peppers
¼ cup finely chopped drained
canned pimiento
1 tablespoon capers
2 teaspoons tarragon vinegar

1½ teaspoons Worcestershire
sauce
¼ teaspoon ground hot red pepper
(cayenne)
½ teaspoon salt
1 tablespoon finely chopped fresh
parsley, preferably the flat-leaf
Italian variety
6 six-ounce redfish fillets, each cut
about ¾ inch thick and skinned,
or substitute any firm white fish
fillets of a comparable size

First prepare the sauce in the following manner: In a heavy 8- to 10-inch skillet, melt the butter bits over moderate heat. When the foam begins to subside, add the onions and garlic and, stirring frequently, cook for about 5 minutes, or until they are soft and translucent but not brown.

Add the fish stock, green peppers, pimiento, capers, vinegar, Worcestershire sauce, red pepper and salt. Stirring constantly, bring to a boil over high heat. Then reduce the heat to low and simmer, partially covered, for about 10 minutes, or until the sauce thickens slightly. Remove the skillet from the heat, stir in the parsley and taste for seasoning. Cover the skillet tightly to keep the sauce warm while you broil the fish.

Preheat the broiler to its highest setting. Pat the fish fillets completely dry with paper towels and brush them on both sides with the 2 tablespoons of melted butter. Arrange the fillets side by side on the broiler grid and broil them about 5 inches from the heat for 15 minutes, or until the fish flakes easily when prodded gently with a fork.

With a wide metal spatula, transfer the fillets to a heated platter. Reheat the sauce briefly, pour it over the fish and serve at once.

Baked Stuffed Redfish

To serve 6 to 8

3 tablespoons vegetable oil
6 tablespoons butter
1 cup soft fresh crumbs made from French- or Italian-type white bread, pulverized in a blender
1 dozen shucked medium-sized oysters, defrosted if frozen, and patted completely dry with paper towels
½ cup finely chopped scallions, including 3 inches of the green tops
¼ cup finely chopped fresh parsley, preferably the flat-leaf Italian variety
1¼ teaspoons crumbled dried thyme

½ teaspoon ground hot red pepper (cayenne)
1½ teaspoons salt
2 medium-sized bay leaves, finely crumbled
½ teaspoon ground cloves
A 5- to 6-pound redfish or red snapper, cleaned but with the head and tail intact
2 cups dry white wine
1 cup finely chopped onions
¼ pound firm fresh mushrooms, trimmed, wiped with a dampened cloth and cut lengthwise, including the stems, into ¼-inch-thick slices
2 one-pound cans tomatoes, drained and coarsely chopped

Preheat the oven to 400°. With a pastry brush, spread 1 tablespoon of the oil over the bottom of a shallow heatproof baking pan large enough to hold the fish comfortably in one layer. Line the pan with a long sheet of heavy-duty aluminum foil and brush the surface of the foil evenly with another tablespoon of oil. Set the lined pan aside.

In a heavy 8- to 10-inch skillet, melt 3 tablespoons of the butter over moderate heat. When the foam begins to subside, add the bread crumbs and stir until they are crisp and golden brown. With a rubber spatula, scrape the entire contents of the skillet into a bowl. Add the oysters, scallions, parsley, ¼ teaspoon of the thyme, ¼ teaspoon of the red pepper and ½ teaspoon of the salt. Toss the ingredients together gently but thoroughly and set the stuffing mixture aside.

Combine the remaining teaspoon of thyme, the bay leaves and the cloves in a bowl and mix well. Wash the fish briefly under cold running water and pat it completely dry with paper towels. Season the cavity of the fish with ½ teaspoon of the remaining salt, then spoon the stuffing mixture into the cavity. Close the opening with small skewers and cord, as if lacing a turkey, or sew it shut with heavy white thread.

Score the skin of the fish by cutting three diagonal slashes about 2 inches long and 2 inches apart in each side. With your fingers, press a little of the thyme and bay leaf mixture into the cuts, dividing the seasonings equally among them.

Place the fish in the lined pan and brush the top with the remaining tablespoon of oil. Pour the wine down the sides of the pan and bring to a simmer on top of the stove. Then bake uncovered on the middle shelf of the oven for about 40 minutes, or until the fish feels firm when prodded gently with a finger.

Meanwhile, prepare the sauce in the following manner: In a heavy 10- to 12-inch skillet, melt the remaining 3 tablespoons of butter over moderate heat. When the foam subsides, add the onions and mushrooms and, stirring frequently, cook for about 5 minutes, or until the onions are soft and translucent but not brown. Stir in the tomatoes, the remaining ¼ teaspoon of red pepper and ½ teaspoon of salt, and bring to a boil over high heat. Still stirring occasionally, cook briskly until most of the liquid in the skillet has evaporated and the tomato sauce is thick enough to hold its shape almost solidly in the spoon. Set the skillet aside off the heat.

When the fish has cooked its allotted time, remove it from the oven. Carefully lift the foil and fish from the pan, using the long ends of the foil as handles, and gently slide the fish onto a heated platter.

Strain the juices remaining in the baking pan through a fine sieve set over a bowl. Pour the strained juice into the reserved tomato sauce and, stirring constantly, bring to a simmer over moderate heat. Taste for seasoning, pour the sauce over the fish and serve at once.

Bouillabaisse, Creole-Style

To serve 4 to 6

2 large garlic cloves, peeled and
   coarsely chopped
3 fresh parsley sprigs, coarsely
   chopped
1 teaspoon crumbled dried thyme
1 small bay leaf, crumbled
½ teaspoon ground allspice
1½ teaspoons salt
5 tablespoons vegetable oil
2½ pounds redfish or red snapper
   fillets, with skin intact, cut into
   6 equal portions
12 medium-sized uncooked shrimp

(about ½ pound)
1 cup finely chopped onions
A 1-pound can tomatoes, drained
   and coarsely chopped
2 cups freshly made fish stock *(page 6)*
¼ teaspoon crumbled dried saffron
   threads or ¼ teaspoon ground
   saffron
¼ teaspoon ground hot red pepper
   (cayenne)
12 medium-sized shucked oysters
   (about ½ pint)
4 to 6 cups freshly cooked white
   rice

With a mortar and pestle or in a small bowl with the back of a spoon, crush the garlic, parsley, thyme, bay leaf, allspice and ½ teaspoon of the salt to a smooth paste, then stir in 2 tablespoons of the oil.

Pat the fish fillets dry with paper towels and sprinkle them with the remaining teaspoon of salt. Spread the garlic paste over the flesh side of each fillet, dividing it evenly among them, and set the fish aside.

Shell the shrimp. Devein them by making a shallow incision down their backs with a small sharp knife and lifting out the black or white intestinal vein with the point of the knife. Wash the shrimp briefly in a colander set under cold running water and put them aside to drain.

In a heavy 12-inch skillet, heat the remaining 3 tablespoons of oil over moderate heat until a light haze forms above it. Add the onions and, stirring frequently, cook for about 5 minutes, or until they are soft and translucent but not brown. Place the fish fillets, skin side down, on top of the onions, cover the skillet tightly and cook over moderate heat for 5 minutes, or until the fish is firm and opaque. With a wide metal spatula, transfer the fillets to a plate and reserve them.

Add the tomatoes, fish stock, saffron and red pepper to the onion mixture remaining in the skillet and bring to a boil over high heat. Stirring occasionally, cook briskly until the sauce is reduced to about 2 cups and is thick enough to hold its shape lightly in the spoon.

Return the fish fillets to the skillet, add the oysters and shrimp, and spoon the sauce over the seafood to moisten it evenly. Reduce the heat to low, cover the skillet tightly and simmer for about 5 minutes, or until the shrimp are pink and firm to the touch and the oysters plump up and begin to curl at the edges.

Taste for seasoning. With a slotted spatula or spoon, arrange the fish fillets, shrimp and oysters attractively on a deep heated platter. Pour the sauce remaining in the skillet over the seafood and serve at once, accompanied by the rice in a separate bowl.

Teal Ducks in Port Wine Sauce

To serve 4

4 eight-ounce oven-ready teal ducks
1 teaspoon salt
½ teaspoon freshly ground black
  pepper
6 tablespoons butter, melted
1 tablespoon flour

½ cup port
½ cup chicken stock, fresh or
  canned
1 teaspoon strained fresh lemon
  juice
2 tablespoons finely grated lemon
  peel

Preheat the oven to 400°. Wash the ducks briefly under cold running water and pat them dry, inside and out, with paper towels. Season the cavities and skin of the ducks with the salt and pepper.

Place the birds on their right sides on a rack set in a shallow roasting pan. With a pastry brush, spread 2 tablespoons of the melted butter evenly over the ducks and roast them in the middle of the oven for 10 minutes. Turn the birds over on their left sides, brush them with 2 more tablespoons of melted butter and roast for 10 minutes longer. Then turn the ducks breast side up, brush them with the remaining melted butter and continue to roast for 10 to 15 minutes more, or until the drumsticks feel soft to the touch and the juices that run out of their vents are clear yellow. Transfer the ducks to a heated platter and drape them with foil to keep them warm while you prepare the sauce.

With a metal spatula, scrape up 1 tablespoon of the brown drippings remaining in the roasting pan and transfer them to a small saucepan set over low heat. Add the flour to the drippings and mix well. Stirring constantly with a wire whisk, pour in the port and chicken stock in slow, thin streams and cook over high heat until the sauce comes to a boil, thickens lightly and is smooth. Reduce the heat to low and simmer for 2 or 3 minutes to remove the raw taste of the flour.

Stir in the lemon juice and taste the sauce for seasoning. Pour the sauce over the ducks, sprinkle the tops with the lemon peel, and serve at once.

Braised Pintail Duck

To serve 4

Two 1½-pound oven-ready pintail
  ducks, with the necks, gizzards
  and hearts reserved
1 teaspoon salt
¼ teaspoon freshly ground black
  pepper
2 tablespoons flour
6 slices lean bacon
2 medium-sized onions, peeled and
  sliced crosswise into ¼-inch-
  thick rounds
½ cup dry red wine
½ cup chicken stock, fresh or
  canned
4 medium-sized carrots, scraped and
  sliced crosswise into ¼-inch-
  thick rounds
¼ teaspoon crumbled dried sage
  leaves
¼ teaspoon finely grated fresh
  lemon peel
⅛ teaspoon crumbled dried thyme

Wash the ducks and giblets (the necks, gizzards and hearts) under cold running water and pat them completely dry with paper towels. Season the cavities of the birds with the salt and pepper and rub the flour into their skin. Truss the ducks neatly.

In a heavy 10-inch skillet, fry the bacon over moderate heat, turning the slices frequently with tongs until they are crisp and brown and have rendered all their fat. Transfer the bacon to paper towels to drain, crumble the slices into small bits, and set them aside.

Add the duck necks, gizzards and hearts to the fat remaining in the pan and, turning them frequently, fry over moderate heat until they are richly browned. With a slotted spoon, transfer the giblets to a heavy 6- to 7-quart casserole.

Then brown the ducks in the bacon fat, turning them with tongs or a spoon and regulating the heat so that they color deeply and evenly without burning. Transfer the birds to the casserole and add the onions to the fat remaining in the skillet. Stirring occasionally, cook over moderate heat for 8 to 10 minutes, or until the onions are soft and brown. With a slotted spoon, add the onions to the ducks.

Pour off the fat remaining in the skillet, add the wine and stock, and bring to a boil over high heat, meanwhile scraping in the brown particles that cling to the bottom and sides of the pan. Stir in the carrots, sage, lemon peel and thyme, and pour the entire contents of the skillet over the ducks. Scatter the reserved bacon bits on top.

Bring the casserole to a boil over high heat, reduce the heat to low, and simmer tightly covered for 1 hour, or until the birds are tender and a thigh shows no resistance when pierced with the point of a small sharp knife.

Taste for seasoning and serve at once, directly from the casserole. Or, if you prefer, arrange the ducks side by side on a deep heated platter and ladle the carrots, onions and cooking liquid over them.

Sausage-stuffed Mallard Ducks

To serve 4

4 tablespoons butter
4 to 5 thin slices homemade-type
white bread, cut into ¼-inch
cubes (about 2 cups)
½ pound (about 1 cup) freshly
made *chaurice (page 84)*,
skinned and crumbled, or
substitute ½ pound hot spicy
Italian sausage meat

½ cup finely chopped onions
½ cup finely chopped celery
½ cup finely chopped peeled apple
1½ teaspoons salt
⅛ teaspoon ground hot red pepper
(cayenne)
Two 1½-pound oven-ready
mallard ducks
4 slices bacon

Preheat the oven to 400°. To make the stuffing, melt the butter in a heavy 8- to 10-inch skillet set over moderate heat. When the foam begins to subside, drop in the bread cubes and stir them about until they are crisp and golden brown. With a slotted spoon, transfer the cubes to a deep bowl.

Place the sausage meat in the skillet and, mashing it frequently to break up any lumps, cook over moderate heat until no trace of pink remains and the meat has rendered all its fat. Do not let the sausage brown. Using the slotted spoon, add the sausage to the toasted bread cubes.

Add the onions and celery to the fat remaining in the skillet and, stirring frequently, cook for about 5 minutes, or until the vegetables are soft but not brown. With a rubber spatula, scrape the entire contents of the skillet into the bowl with the sausage and bread cubes. Add the apple, ½ teaspoon of the salt and the red pepper, and toss the stuffing ingredients together gently but thoroughly. Taste for seasoning.

Wash the mallards briefly under cold running water and pat them dry, inside and out, with paper towels. Rub the skin of the birds with the remaining teaspoon of salt. Then fill the cavities with the sausage stuffing and close the openings by lacing them with cord and small skewers or sewing them with heavy white thread. Truss the mallards neatly.

Cross two bacon slices over the breast of each duck and wrap the ends of the bacon under the birds, pressing the slices snugly against the bodies to keep them in place. Place the ducks breast side up on a rack set in a shallow roasting pan, and roast in the middle of the oven for 10 minutes. Then reduce the oven temperature to 350° and continue roasting for 30 minutes longer. To test for doneness, pierce a thigh with the point of a small sharp knife. The juice that trickles out should be clear yellow; if it is still tinged with pink, roast the ducks for another 5 to 10 minutes.

Transfer the sausage-stuffed mallards to a heated platter and, for easier carving, let them rest for about 10 minutes before serving.

Duck Jambalaya

To serve 4

A 4½- to 5-pound duck, trimmed
    of excess fat and cut into
    8 serving pieces
1 teaspoon ground hot red pepper
    (cayenne)
1 teaspoon salt
½ cup flour
2 tablespoons vegetable oil
1 cup finely chopped onions
½ teaspoon finely chopped garlic

4 cups chicken stock, fresh or
    canned
2 cups coarsely chopped drained
    canned tomatoes
2 cups uncooked white rice,
    preferably broken rice (see
    Glossary, page 150)
1 cup finely chopped scallions,
    including 3 inches of the green
    tops

Pat the pieces of duck completely dry with paper towels and season them on all sides with the red pepper and salt. Roll one piece at a time in the flour to coat it evenly and vigorously shake off the excess flour.

In a heavy 4- to 5-quart casserole, heat the oil over moderate heat until a light haze forms above it. Brown the duck in the hot oil, four pieces at a time to avoid overcrowding the pan. Turn the pieces frequently with tongs and regulate the heat so that they color richly and evenly without burning. As they brown, transfer the pieces to a plate.

Pour off all but about 3 tablespoons of the fat remaining in the casserole and add the onions and garlic. Stirring frequently, cook over moderate heat for about 5 minutes, or until the onions are soft and translucent but not brown. Stir in 2 cups of the chicken stock and the tomatoes, and bring to a boil over high heat, meanwhile scraping in the brown particles that cling to the bottom and sides of the pan.

Return the duck to the casserole, reduce the heat to low, and simmer partially covered for 1 hour 15 minutes. Stir in the remaining 2 cups of chicken stock and the rice, and bring the mixture to a boil. Reduce the heat to low, cover tightly, and simmer for about 20 minutes, or until the rice is tender and the grains have absorbed all the liquid.

Add the scallions, then fluff the rice with a table fork. Taste for seasoning and serve the duck jambalaya at once, directly from the casserole or from a large heated bowl.

Louisiana Chicken

To serve 4

A 2½- to 3-pound chicken, cut into 8 serving pieces
½ teaspoon salt
½ teaspoon ground hot red pepper (cayenne)
½ cup vegetable oil
4 tablespoons butter
¾ pound fresh mushrooms, trimmed, wiped with a dampened cloth, and finely chopped (about 4 cups)
¼ cup flour
2 cups chicken stock, fresh or canned
¼ cup thinly sliced pitted green olives
¼ cup dry sherry
A 10-ounce package frozen artichoke hearts, freshly cooked

Pat the pieces of chicken completely dry with paper towels and season them on all sides with the salt and red pepper. In a heavy 12-inch skillet, heat the oil over moderate heat until a light haze forms above it. Fry the chicken in the hot oil, starting the pieces skin side down and turning them frequently with tongs for about 20 minutes, or until they brown richly and evenly. To be sure that the bird is cooked to the proper degree of doneness, lift a thigh from the pan and pierce it deeply with the point of a small skewer or sharp knife. The juice that trickles out should be clear yellow; if it is still tinged with pink, fry the chicken for 2 or 3 minutes more. As they are cooked, drain the pieces of chicken briefly on paper towels. Then arrange them on a heated platter and drape them with foil to keep them warm.

Meanwhile, in another large heavy skillet, melt the butter over moderate heat. When the foam subsides, add the mushrooms and, stirring occasionally, cook for 5 minutes, or until the mushrooms are tender and the liquid that accumulates in the pan has evaporated. Do not let the mushrooms brown. Remove the pan from the heat and reserve the mushrooms.

When the chicken has cooked its allotted time and been transferred to the platter, pour off all but about 4 tablespoons of the fat remaining in the skillet and in its place add the flour; mix well. Stirring constantly with a wire whisk, pour in the chicken stock in a slow, thin stream and cook over high heat until the sauce comes to a boil, thickens heavily and is smooth. Reduce the heat to low and simmer for 2 or 3 minutes to remove the raw taste of the flour.

Stir in the mushrooms, olives, sherry and artichoke hearts, and simmer for a minute or so longer to heat them through. Taste for seasoning, then ladle the sauce and vegetables over the chicken and serve at once.

Chicken Rochambeau

CHICKEN AND HAM ON RUSKS WITH MUSHROOM AND BÉARNAISE SAUCES

To serve 4

MUSHROOM SAUCE
2 tablespoons butter
1 cup finely chopped scallions,
   including 3 inches of the green
   tops
1 teaspoon finely chopped garlic
2 tablespoons flour
2 cups chicken stock, fresh or

canned
½ cup finely chopped fresh
   mushrooms (¼ pound)
½ cup dry red wine
1 tablespoon Worcestershire sauce
⅛ teaspoon ground hot red pepper
   (cayenne)
½ teaspoon salt

This elegant chicken dish is said to be named for Count Jean Baptiste Donatien de Vimeur de Rochambeau, who commanded the French forces that supported Washington in the American Revolution.

First prepare the mushroom sauce in the following fashion: In a heavy 1- to 1½-quart saucepan, melt the 2 tablespoons of butter over moderate heat. When the foam begins to subside, add the cup of scallions and the garlic and stir for about 5 minutes, or until they are soft but not brown. Add 2 tablespoons of flour and mix well. Stirring constantly with a wire whisk, pour in the chicken stock in a slow, thin stream and cook over high heat until the sauce comes to a boil, thickens lightly and is smooth.

Stir in the mushrooms, reduce the heat to low and simmer partially covered for about 15 minutes, until the mushrooms are tender but still intact. Then add the wine, Worcestershire, ⅛ teaspoon of red pepper and ½ teaspoon of salt, and stir over low heat for 2 or 3 minutes. Taste for seasoning, remove from the heat and cover tightly to keep the sauce warm.

CHICKEN
2 one-pound chicken breasts, boned
   and halved but with the skin
   intact
1 teaspoon salt

½ teaspoon freshly ground black
   pepper
½ cup flour
12 tablespoons butter, cut into
   ½-inch bits

Pat the chicken breasts completely dry with paper towels and season them on all sides with the teaspoon of salt and the black pepper. Roll one piece of chicken breast at a time in the ½ cup of flour and, when evenly coated, shake vigorously to remove the excess flour.

Melt 12 tablespoons of butter bits in a heavy 10- to 12-inch skillet set over moderate heat. Do not let the butter brown. When the foam subsides, add the chicken breasts skin side down and, turning the pieces occasionally with tongs, cook over moderate heat until they are lightly brown on all sides. Reduce the heat to low, cover the skillet tightly and simmer the chicken for about 20 minutes, until it is tender and shows no resistance when pierced deeply with the point of a small sharp knife. As it simmers use a bulb baster or a large spoon to baste the chicken every 7 or 8 minutes with the pan juices.

HAM
1 teaspoon butter
Four ¼-inch-thick slices Canadian
bacon or lean cooked smoked
ham
4 Holland rusks

Meanwhile preheat the oven to its lowest setting. In another large skillet, melt 1 teaspoon of butter over moderate heat and brown the ham. Turn the slices with tongs and regulate the heat so that they color richly and evenly on both sides without burning. When they brown, arrange the ham slices in one layer on a large baking sheet, drape loosely with foil and keep them warm in the oven. Place the Holland rusks side by side on another baking sheet and put them in the oven to warm.

BÉARNAISE SAUCE
⅔ cup tarragon vinegar
¼ cup finely chopped scallions
1 teaspoon crumbled dried tarragon
4 sprigs fresh parsley
¼ teaspoon whole peppercorns
12 tablespoons butter, cut into
    ½-inch bits
4 egg yolks
1 tablespoon water
2 tablespoons strained fresh lemon
    juice
¼ teaspoon ground hot red pepper
    (cayenne)
½ teaspoon salt

About 10 minutes before the chicken is done, make the béarnaise sauce. Combine the vinegar, ¼ cup of scallions, tarragon, parsley and peppercorns in a small enameled or stainless-steel saucepan. Bring to a boil over high heat and cook briskly, uncovered, until reduced to about 2 tablespoons. Strain the liquid through a fine sieve into a small bowl, pressing down hard on the seasonings with the back of a spoon to extract all their juices before discarding the pulp. Set the strained liquid aside.

In a heavy 8- to 10-inch skillet, melt the 12 tablespoons of butter bits over low heat, stirring so that the butter melts evenly without browning. Remove the pan from the heat and cover to keep the melted butter warm.

Working quickly, combine the egg yolks and water in a 1½- to 2-quart enameled or stainless-steel saucepan, and beat with a wire whisk until the mixture is foamy. Then place the pan over the lowest possible heat and continue whisking until the mixture thickens and almost doubles in volume. Do not let it come anywhere near a boil or the yolks will curdle; if necessary, lift the pan off the heat from time to time to cool it.

Still whisking constantly, pour in the reserved hot melted butter as slowly as possible and beat over low heat until the sauce thickens heavily. Beat in the reserved strained liquid, the lemon juice, ¼ teaspoon of red pepper and the salt, and taste for seasoning. Set it aside off the heat.

Before assembling the chicken Rochambeau, stir the mushroom sauce briefly and warm it over low heat if necessary. Arrange the rusks on a large heated platter or four individual serving plates. Place a slice of ham on each rusk and spoon the mushroom sauce over the slices, dividing it equally among them. Set a chicken breast on top of each ham slice and ladle 2 or 3 tablespoons of béarnaise over it. Pour the remaining béarnaise into a sauceboat and serve it at once with the chicken Rochambeau.

Chicken Pontalba

CHICKEN BREAST ON A BED OF HAM AND POTATOES WITH BÉARNAISE SAUCE

To serve 4

14 tablespoons plus ½ pound butter, all cut into ½-inch bits

1 medium-sized onion, peeled and cut crosswise into ⅛-inch-thick slices

½ cup finely chopped fresh mushrooms

½ cup finely chopped scallions, including 3 inches of the green tops

1 tablespoon finely chopped garlic

¼ pound cooked smoked ham, sliced ¼ inch thick and cut into ¼-inch dice

½ cup dry white wine

2 tablespoons finely chopped parsley plus 4 fresh parsley sprigs, both preferably the flat-leaf Italian variety

2 one-pound chicken breasts, skinned, boned and halved

1 teaspoon salt

¼ teaspoon freshly ground black pepper

½ cup flour

1 tablespoon vegetable oil plus vegetable oil for deep frying

1 large boiling potato, peeled and cut into ¼-inch dice

⅔ cup tarragon vinegar

1 teaspoon crumbled dried tarragon

10 whole black peppercorns

4 egg yolks

1 tablespoon water

2 tablespoons strained fresh lemon juice

¼ teaspoon ground hot red pepper (cayenne)

This elaborate chicken assemblage takes its name from the historic Pontalba Buildings in the French Quarter of New Orleans. This apartment complex, one of the earliest in America, was built in the 1840s by Michaela, Baroness Pontalba, the daughter of Don Andrés Almonester y Roxas—an altruistic Spanish grandee who financed the building of New Orleans' Saint Louis Cathedral, where he is buried.

First prepare the ham mixture in the following manner: In a heavy 8- to 10-inch skillet, melt 2 tablespoons of the butter bits over moderate heat. When the foam begins to subside, add the onion, the mushrooms, ¼ cup of the scallions and the garlic. Stirring frequently, cook for about 5 minutes, or until the vegetables are soft but not brown and the liquid that accumulates in the pan has evaporated. Add the ham and stir until the mixture browns delicately. Then add the wine and chopped parsley and, stirring constantly, cook briskly until the mixture is thick enough to hold its shape almost solidly in the spoon. Remove the skillet from the heat and cover to keep the ham mixture warm.

Pat the chicken breasts dry with paper towels and season them on all sides with ½ teaspoon of the salt and the black pepper. Roll one piece of chicken at a time in the flour to coat it lightly, and vigorously shake off the excess flour.

Melt 8 tablespoons of the butter bits with 1 tablespoon of vegetable oil in a heavy 10- to 12-inch skillet set over moderate heat, stirring so that the butter does not brown. When the foam subsides, add the chicken breasts and, turning the pieces occasionally, cook over moderate heat until they are lightly and evenly browned. Reduce the heat to low, cover the skillet tightly and simmer the chicken for about 20 minutes, until it is tender and shows no resistance when pierced deeply with the point of a small sharp knife. As it simmers, use a bulb baster or a large spoon to baste the chicken every 7 or 8 minutes with the pan juices.

Meanwhile, preheat the oven to its lowest setting. Line a shallow baking dish with a double thickness of paper towels and place it on the middle shelf of the oven.

Pour vegetable oil into a deep fryer or large heavy saucepan to a depth of 2 or 3 inches and heat the oil until it reaches a temperature of 375° on a deep-frying thermometer. Pat the diced potato completely dry with paper towels, place the dice in a large sieve and lower the sieve into the hot oil. Stirring the dice with a skimmer or slotted spoon, deep-fry them for 2 or 3 minutes, until they color lightly and evenly. Transfer the potato to the paper-lined dish and keep it warm in the oven.

About 10 minutes before the chicken is done, make the béarnaise. Combine the vinegar, the remaining ¼ cup of scallions, the tarragon, parsley sprigs and peppercorns in a small enameled or stainless-steel saucepan. Bring to a boil over high heat and cook briskly, uncovered, until reduced to about 2 tablespoons. Strain the liquid through a fine sieve into a small bowl, pressing down hard on the seasonings with the back of a spoon to extract all their juices before discarding the pulp. Set the liquid aside.

In a small heavy pan, melt the remaining ½ pound plus 4 tablespoons of butter bits over low heat. Do not let the butter brown. Remove the pan from the heat and cover to keep the butter warm.

Working quickly, combine the egg yolks and water in a 1½- to 2-quart enameled or stainless-steel saucepan, and beat vigorously with a wire whisk until the mixture is foamy. Then place the pan over the lowest possible heat and continue whisking until the mixture thickens and almost doubles in volume. Do not let the yolks come anywhere near a boil or they will curdle; if necessary, lift the pan off the heat from time to time to let it cool for a few moments.

Still whisking constantly, pour in the reserved warm melted butter as slowly as possible and continue to beat over low heat until the sauce thickens heavily. Beat in the lemon juice, red pepper and the remaining ½ teaspoon of salt, and then taste the béarnaise for seasoning. Set the sauce aside off the heat.

Before assembling the chicken Pontalba, add the deep-fried potatoes to the ham mixture and stir over moderate heat for a minute or so to blend the mixture and heat it through. Spoon the mixture onto four individual heated serving plates, dividing it evenly among them, and smooth the top with the back of the spoon. Place a chicken breast half on each portion and ladle the béarnaise over it. Serve at once.

Quail Pontalba

QUAIL WITH ORANGE-LIQUEUR SAUCE

To serve 6

6 four-ounce oven-ready quail
1 teaspoon salt
½ teaspoon freshly ground black
  pepper
½ cup flour
2 tablespoons butter

¼ cup vegetable oil
1½ cups dry white wine
3 oranges
2 teaspoons cornstarch combined
  with ½ cup curaçao or other
  orange-flavored liqueur
½ cup coarsely chopped walnuts

Like chicken Pontalba, this quail dish takes its name from the Pontalba Buildings, a New Orleans landmark. Though both recipes feature fowl, they are not similar in any other way.

Pat the quail completely dry, inside and out, with paper towels and season their cavities and skin with the salt and pepper. Truss the birds neatly, then roll one at a time in the flour to coat it lightly, and vigorously shake off the excess flour.

In a heavy 10- to 12-inch skillet, melt the butter with the oil over moderate heat. When the foam begins to subside, brown the birds, turning them frequently with tongs and regulating the heat so that they color richly and evenly on all sides without burning. As they brown, transfer the quail to a plate.

Pour the wine into the fat remaining in the skillet and bring to a boil over high heat, meanwhile scraping in the brown particles that cling to the bottom and sides of the pan. Return the quail and the liquid that has accumulated around them to the skillet and baste the birds well with the wine. Reduce the heat to low, cover tightly, and simmer for about 30 minutes, or until a drumstick feels soft when prodded gently with a finger.

Meanwhile, using a small sharp knife or swivel-bladed vegetable parer, remove the peel from the oranges without cutting into the bitter white pith underneath. Cut the peel into strips about 1½ inches long and ¼ inch wide; drop the strips into enough boiling water to immerse them completely and boil briskly, uncovered, for 1 or 2 minutes. Drain the strips of blanched peel in a sieve and spread them on paper towels to dry.

With a small, very sharp knife, use short sawing motions to cut all the white pith and membrane from two of the oranges. (Set the third orange aside for another use.) To section the two oranges, cut along each side of each membrane division to the core of the orange. As each orange section is freed, carefully lift it out and place it on paper towels to drain.

When the quail have cooked for their allotted time, transfer them to a heated platter and drape foil over them to keep them warm while you prepare the sauce. Stirring constantly with a wire whisk, pour the cornstarch-and-liqueur mixture gradually into the liquid remaining in the skillet and cook over moderate heat until the sauce thickens lightly and is smooth. Stir in the reserved orange peel, the orange sections and the walnuts, and cook for a minute or so to heat them through. Taste the sauce for seasoning, ladle it over the quail and serve at once.

Pigeon Casserole

To serve 2

2 one-pound oven-ready squab pigeons	¼ cup flour
½ teaspoon ground hot red pepper (cayenne)	2 cups chicken stock, fresh or canned
1 teaspoon salt	½ cup dry red wine
2 tablespoons butter	¼ pound firm fresh mushrooms, trimmed, wiped with a dampened towel and cut lengthwise, including the stems, into ¼-inch-thick slices
2 tablespoons vegetable oil	
½ cup finely chopped onions	
½ cup finely chopped celery	
2 medium-sized carrots, scraped and thinly sliced	½ cup fresh or thoroughly defrosted frozen Lima beans
¼ cup finely chopped scallions, including 3 inches of the green tops	2 tablespoons finely chopped fresh parsley, preferably the flat-leaf Italian variety

Wash the pigeons briefly under cold running water and pat them completely dry, inside and out, with paper towels. Season the cavities and skin of the birds with ¼ teaspoon of the red pepper and ½ teaspoon of the salt, then truss them neatly.

In a heavy 4- to 5-quart casserole, melt the butter with the oil over moderate heat. When the foam begins to subside, place the pigeons in the casserole and brown them, turning the birds about with a spoon and regulating the heat so that they color richly and evenly on all sides without burning. Transfer the birds to a plate and set them aside.

Add the onions, celery, carrots and scallions to the fat remaining in the casserole and, stirring frequently, cook for 8 to 10 minutes, or until the vegetables are soft and delicately browned. Add the flour and mix well. Stirring constantly, pour in the chicken stock and the red wine in a slow, thin stream and cook over high heat until the sauce mixture comes to a boil and thickens lightly.

Stir in the mushrooms, Lima beans and the remaining ¼ teaspoon of red pepper and ½ teaspoon of salt. Return the pigeons and the liquid that has accumulated around them to the casserole and turn the birds about with a spoon to coat them evenly with the sauce and vegetables.

Reduce the heat to low and partially cover the casserole. Turning the birds from time to time, simmer for about 45 minutes, or until they are tender and a thigh shows no resistance when pierced deeply with the point of a small sharp knife.

Taste for seasoning, add the parsley and serve at once, directly from the casserole or from a large heated bowl.

Creole Boiled Beef

To serve 8

2 tablespoons vegetable oil
A 4- to 4½-pound lean fresh beef brisket, trimmed of all excess fat, rolled and tied
6 quarts cold water
3 large onions, peeled and coarsely chopped
3 large garlic cloves, peeled and coarsely chopped
2 medium-sized carrots, scraped and coarsely chopped, plus 6 medium-sized carrots, scraped and cut lengthwise into quarters
2 medium-sized firm ripe tomatoes, peeled, seeded and coarsely chopped (see shrimp Creole, page 51)
1 cup coarsely chopped celery leaves
1 medium-sized turnip, scraped and coarsely chopped
1 medium-sized parsnip, scraped and coarsely chopped
1 small hot red dried chili, stemmed, seeded and coarsely crumbled (caution: see note, page 6)
1 large bay leaf
2 or 3 fresh parsley sprigs, preferably the flat-leaf Italian variety
½ teaspoon crumbled dried thyme
6 whole allspice
10 whole black peppercorns
1 tablespoon salt
A 1- to 1½-pound green cabbage, trimmed, cut lengthwise into 8 wedges, and cored
16 small boiling potatoes, peeled

In a heavy 12-inch skillet, heat the vegetable oil over moderate heat until a light haze forms above it. Pat the brisket of beef completely dry with paper towels and brown it in the hot oil. Turn the brisket frequently with two large spoons and regulate the heat so that it colors deeply and evenly on all sides without burning. Transfer the beef to a heavy 10- to 12-quart pot and pour the water over it. Bring to a boil over high heat and skim off the foam and scum as they rise to the surface.

Meanwhile, discard all but 2 tablespoons of the fat remaining in the skillet. Add the onions, garlic and chopped carrots and, stirring frequently, cook over moderate heat for 8 to 10 minutes, or until the vegetables are soft and delicately browned. With a slotted spoon, transfer the vegetable mixture to the pot with the beef.

Stir in the tomatoes, celery leaves, turnip, parsnip, chili, bay leaf, parsley, thyme, allspice, peppercorns and salt, and return the liquid to a boil. Reduce the heat to low, cover the pot partially, and simmer for 2½ hours, or until the brisket is almost tender and shows only slight resistance when pierced deeply with the point of a small sharp knife.

Transfer the brisket to a plate and set aside. Strain the stock through a fine sieve lined with cheesecloth and set over a bowl. Discard the vegetables and seasonings, skim the fat from the stock, and taste for seasoning.

Wash the pot and return the brisket and stock to it. Add the quartered carrots, cabbage and potatoes, and bring to a boil over high heat. Cook briskly, uncovered, for about 20 minutes, until the meat and vegetables are tender. Then transfer the meat to a cutting board, remove the strings and carve the brisket into ¼-inch-thick slices. Arrange the slices attractively on a heated platter, overlapping them slightly, and place the carrots, cabbage wedges and potatoes around them. Serve the meat and vegetables accompanied by cupfuls of the stock or, if you prefer, serve the meat, vegetables and stock together in heated soup plates.

Boiled-Beef Sausage

To make 2 sausages, each about 30 inches long

2 three-foot lengths of hog sausage casing
6 cups leftover Creole boiled beef (*opposite*), coarsely chopped
½ pound lean boneless pork, cut into small chunks
½ pound fresh pork fat

½ cup beef stock, fresh or canned
¼ cup dry sherry
¼ cup finely chopped fresh parsley, preferably the flat-leaf Italian variety
2 teaspoons finely chopped garlic
½ teaspoon ground allspice
½ teaspoon ground hot red pepper (cayenne)
1 teaspoon salt

Place the sausage casing in a bowl, pour in enough warm water to cover it by 1 inch, and soak 2 or 3 hours, until the casing is soft and pliable.

Put the boiled beef, pork and pork fat through the coarsest blade of a food grinder and transfer the mixture to a bowl. Add the beef stock, sherry, parsley, garlic, allspice, red pepper and salt. Knead the ingredients vigorously together with both hands, then beat with a wooden spoon until the mixture is smooth and fluffy.

Wash the sausage casing thoroughly but gently under cold, slowly running water to remove all traces of the salt in which it was preserved. Hold one end securely around the faucet and let the cold water run through to rinse the inside of the casing.

To make each sausage, tie a knot about 3 inches from the end of one length of casing. Fit the open end snugly over the funnel (or "horn") on the sausage-making attachment of a meat grinder. Then ease the rest of the casing up onto the funnel, squeezing it together like the folds of an accordion. Spoon the meat mixture into the mouth of the funnel and, with a wooden pestle, push it through into the casing.

As you fill it, the casing will expand and gradually ease away from the funnel in a coil. Fill the casing to within an inch or so of the open end; do not stuff it too tight or it may burst. Slip the casing off the funnel and knot the open end. If you do not cook the sausages immediately, you may refrigerate them safely for 5 or 6 days.

NOTE: Before cooking a sausage, prick the casing in five or six places with the point of a skewer or a small knife. Coil the sausage in concentric circles in a heavy 10- to 12-inch skillet and pour in enough water to cover it completely. Bring to a simmer over moderate heat, then simmer uncovered for about 20 minutes, or until the liquid in the pan has evaporated and only the fat given up by the sausage remains. Add 3 tablespoons of vegetable oil or 2 tablespoons of oil and 1 tablespoon of butter to the skillet and reduce the heat to low. Turning the sausage once or twice with tongs, fry for about 10 minutes, or until it is brown on both sides.

Chaurice

SPICY PORK SAUSAGE

To make 3 sausages, each about
    30 inches long

3 three-foot lengths of hog sausage
    casing
4 pounds lean boneless pork,
    trimmed of excess fat and cut into
    1½-inch chunks
2 pounds fresh pork fat
2 cups finely chopped onions
1 cup finely chopped fresh parsley,
    preferably the flat-leaf Italian
    variety
2 tablespoons finely chopped garlic
2 tablespoons finely chopped fresh

hot red chilies *(caution: see note,
    page 6)*
2 teaspoons crushed dried hot red
    pepper
2 teaspoons ground hot red pepper
    (cayenne)
2 teaspoons freshly ground black
    pepper
2 teaspoons ground thyme
½ teaspoon ground allspice
¼ teaspoon saltpeter
1 tablespoon salt

Place the sausage casing in a large bowl, pour in enough warm water to cover it by at least 1 inch, and soak for 2 or 3 hours, until the casing is soft and pliable.

Put the pork and the pork fat through the medium blade of a food grinder and place the mixture in a deep bowl. Add the onions, parsley, garlic, chilies, crushed red pepper, ground red pepper, black pepper, thyme, allspice, saltpeter and salt. Beat vigorously with a wooden spoon until the mixture is smooth and fluffy.

Wash the sausage casing thoroughly but gently under cold, slowly running water to remove all traces of the salt in which it was preserved. Hold one end securely around the faucet and let the cold water run through to clean the inside of the casing.

To make each sausage, tie a knot about 3 inches from one end of a length of the casing. Fit the open end snugly over the funnel (or "horn") on the sausage-making attachment of a meat grinder. Then ease the rest of the casing up onto the funnel, gently squeezing it together like the folds of an accordion.

Spoon the meat mixture into the mouth of the grinder and, with a wooden pestle, push it through into the casing. As you fill it, the sausage casing will inflate and gradually ease away from the funnel in a ropelike coil. Fill the casing to within an inch or so of the funnel end but do not try to stuff it too tightly, or it may burst. Slip the casing off the funnel and knot the open end of the sausage.

You may cook the sausages immediately, or, if you prefer, you may refrigerate them safely for 5 or 6 days.

Before cooking a sausage, prick the casing in five or six places with a skewer or the point of a small sharp knife. Coil the sausage in concentric circles in a heavy 10- to 12-inch skillet and pour in enough water to cover it completely. Then bring to a simmer over moderate heat. Cook uncovered for 30 to 45 minutes, until the liquid in the pan has evaporated and only the fat given up by the sausage remains. Reduce the heat to low and, turning the sausage once or twice with tongs, continue frying for about 10 minutes longer, or until it is brown on both sides.

NOTE: If you do not have a food grinder with a sausage-stuffing attachment, you can prepare sausage meat as a dish in itself. Ask the butcher to grind the pork and the pork fat. Combine the mixture with the seasonings as described above. Then pat and shape the sausage meat into equal cylinders each about 2 inches in diameter. Wrap tightly with foil or plastic wrap and refrigerate for up to 5 or 6 days, or until ready to use.

To cook, slice the sausage into rounds about ½ inch thick, and fry them in a little hot vegetable oil. Test for doneness by piercing the sausage with the point of a knife; the sausage is done when no trace of pink shows in the meat.

Boudin Blanc

To make 3 sausages, each about 30
    inches long

3 three-foot lengths hog sausage
    casing
3 pounds boneless lean pork,
    trimmed of excess fat and cut into
    1½-inch chunks
4 cups coarsely chopped onions
1 medium-sized bay leaf, crumbled
6 whole black peppercorns
5 teaspoons salt
1 cup coarsely chopped green
    pepper

1 cup coarsely chopped fresh
    parsley, preferably the flat-leaf
    Italian variety
½ cup coarsely chopped scallions
1 tablespoon finely chopped garlic
2½ cups freshly cooked white rice
1 tablespoon dried sage leaves
2½ teaspoons ground hot red
    pepper (cayenne)
½ teaspoon freshly ground black
    pepper

Boudin is the French term for the blood sausage, or "pudding," made with the blood of the pig. Boudin blanc is a white sausage made with pork but no blood. This Louisiana version adds rice and is even whiter.

Place the sausage casing in a bowl, pour in enough warm water to cover it, and soak for 2 or 3 hours, until the casing is soft and pliable.

Meanwhile, put the pork in a heavy 4- to 5-quart casserole and add enough water to cover it by 1 inch. Bring to a boil over high heat and skim off the foam and scum that rise to the surface. Add 2 cups of onions, the bay leaf, peppercorns and 1 teaspoon of the salt. Reduce the heat to low and simmer, partially covered, for 1½ hours.

Continued on next page

With a slotted spoon, transfer the chunks of pork to a plate. (Discard the cooking liquid and seasonings.) Put the pork, the remaining 2 cups of onions, the green pepper, parsley, scallions and garlic through the medium blade of a food grinder and place the mixture in a deep bowl. Add the rice, sage, red and black pepper, and the remaining 4 teaspoons of salt. Knead vigorously with both hands, then beat with a wooden spoon until the mixture is smooth and fluffy. Taste for seasoning.

Wash each sausage casing under cold running water to remove all traces of the salt in which it is preserved. Hold one end securely around the faucet and let the water run through to clean the inside of the casing.

To make each sausage, tie a knot 3 inches from one end of a length of the casing. Fit the open end over the funnel (or "horn") on the sausage-making attachment of a meat grinder. Then ease the rest of the casing onto the funnel, squeezing it up like the folds of an accordion.

Spoon the meat mixture into the mouth of the grinder and, with a wooden pestle, push it through into the casing. As you fill it, the casing will inflate and gradually ease away from the funnel in a ropelike coil. Fill the casing to within an inch or so of the funnel end but do not try to stuff it too tightly, or it may burst. Slip the casing off the funnel and knot the open end. You may cook the sausages immediately or refrigerate them safely for five or six days.

Before cooking a sausage, prick the casing in five or six places with a skewer or the point of a small sharp knife. Melt 2 tablespoons of butter with 1 tablespoon of vegetable oil in a heavy 12-inch skillet set over moderate heat. When the foam begins to subside, place the sausage in the skillet, coiling it in concentric circles. Turning the sausage with tongs, cook uncovered for about 10 minutes, or until it is brown on both sides.

Stuffed Ponce

To serve 6

A 1-pound pig's stomach *(ponce)*
3 thin slices homemade-type white
   bread, crusts removed
½ cup milk
2 tablespoons butter
¼ cup finely chopped onions
¼ cup finely chopped green
   peppers
¼ cup finely chopped scallions
1½ teaspoons finely chopped

garlic
1½ pounds lean ground pork
2 medium-sized yams, peeled and
   cut into ¼-inch dice
1 egg
½ teaspoon ground hot red pepper
   (cayenne)
2 teaspoons salt
2 tablespoons vegetable oil
3 to 4 cups water

With your fingers, pick off and discard any bits of fat clinging to the lining or surface of the pig's stomach. Then place the stomach in a deep pot, pour in enough cold water to cover it by at least 1 inch and let it soak for about 2 hours. Rinse the stomach briefly under cold running water and pat it completely dry, inside and out, with paper towels.

Meanwhile, prepare the stuffing in the following manner: Combine the slices of bread and the milk in a bowl and let them stand at room temperature until all the liquid has been absorbed. Place the bread in a sieve and, with the back of a large spoon, press out any excess milk. Discard the milk and set the bread aside.

In a heavy 10-inch skillet, melt the butter over moderate heat. When the foam begins to subside, add the onions, green peppers, scallions and garlic and, stirring frequently, cook for about 5 minutes, or until the vegetables are soft but not brown. With a rubber spatula, scrape the entire contents of the skillet into a deep bowl and let the vegetables cool to room temperature.

When the vegetables are cool, add the reserved bread, the ground pork, yams, egg, red pepper and salt. Knead vigorously with both hands, then beat with a large spoon until the mixture is light and fluffy. Because the stuffing contains raw pork, fry a spoonful of it in a skillet before tasting it for seasoning. With a large needle and strong white thread, sew up one of the openings of the stomach. Then fill the stomach cavity with the stuffing and sew the other opening securely shut.

Heat the oil over moderate heat in a heavy casserole just large enough to hold the stomach comfortably. Add the stuffed *ponce* and turn it over with two wooden spoons until it is lightly browned on all sides. Pour in 1 cup of the water and, when it comes to a boil, cover the casserole tightly. Reduce the heat to moderate and steam the *ponce* for 3 hours, regulating the heat to keep the water at a simmer. Check the casserole every 20 minutes or so and add boiling water as necessary to keep the liquid at a depth of about ½ inch.

Transfer the stuffed *ponce* to a heated platter and let it rest for at least 10 minutes for easier carving. Meanwhile, boil the liquid remaining in the casserole until it is reduced to a thin gravy with the intensity of flavor you desire. Pour the gravy into a bowl and serve it separately. At the table, carve the *ponce* crosswise into ¼-inch-thick slices.

Sausage-and-Eggplant Jambalaya

To serve 4

½ pound freshly made *boudin blanc (page 85)* or boiled-beef sausage *(page 83)*, cut crosswise into ¼-inch-thick slices (about 1 cup), or substitute ½ pound breakfast-type sausages, sliced

½ pound peperoni or other spicy smoked sausage, cut crosswise into ¼-inch-thick slices

½ cup finely chopped onions

¼ cup finely chopped green pepper

¼ cup finely chopped celery

1 teaspoon finely chopped garlic

1¼ cups uncooked white rice, preferably broken rice *(see Glossary, page 150)*

2½ to 3 cups water

½ teaspoon ground hot red pepper (cayenne)

1 tablespoon salt

2 medium-sized eggplants (1 pound each), stemmed, peeled and cut into ½-inch cubes

In a heavy 5- to 6-quart casserole, fry the fresh and smoked sausage slices over moderate heat, turning them frequently with a slotted spatula until they are lightly browned and have rendered all their fat. Transfer the sausage slices to paper towels to drain.

Pour off all but about 4 tablespoons of the fat remaining in the skillet and add the onions, green pepper, celery and garlic. Stirring frequently, cook over moderate heat for about 5 minutes, or until the vegetables are soft but not brown. Add the rice and stir until the grains are evenly moistened. Then add 2½ cups of water, the red pepper and salt, and bring to a boil over high heat.

Stir in the reserved sausage slices and the eggplant, reduce the heat to low, and partially cover the casserole. Simmer for about 45 minutes, or until the eggplant is tender and the rice is soft and somewhat sticky. When fully cooked, most of the liquid in the jambalaya will have evaporated or been absorbed by the rice. While it is simmering, however, check the pot occasionally and add up to ½ cup more water, a few tablespoonfuls at a time, if necessary.

Taste for seasoning and serve the sausage-and-eggplant jambalaya at once, directly from the casserole or from a heated bowl.

Backbone Stew

To serve 8 to 10

A 6-pound lean pork loin, including the bones, sawed into 2-inch chunks
¼ teaspoon ground hot red pepper (cayenne)
1 teaspoon salt
½ cup flour
½ cup vegetable oil

2 cups finely chopped onions
½ cup finely chopped celery plus ¼ cup finely chopped celery leaves
2 tablespoons finely chopped garlic
1 quart chicken stock, fresh or canned
2 fresh parsley sprigs, preferably the flat-leaf Italian variety

Pat the chunks of pork loin completely dry with paper towels and season them on all sides with the red pepper and salt. One at a time, roll the pork chunks in the flour to coat them lightly all over, and vigorously shake off the excess flour.

In a heavy 12-inch skillet, heat the oil over moderate heat until a light haze forms above it. Add the pork and brown the chunks, turning them frequently with kitchen tongs or a metal spatula and regulating the heat so that they color deeply and evenly without burning. Transfer the browned pork chunks to a heavy 8-quart casserole.

Discard all but about ½ cup of the fat remaining in the skillet, and add the onions, the chopped celery (but not the leaves) and the garlic. Stirring from time to time, cook over moderate heat for 8 to 10 minutes, or until the vegetables are lightly browned.

Pour in about ½ cup of the chicken stock and bring to a boil over high heat, meanwhile scraping in the brown particles that cling to the bottom and sides of the skillet.

Pour the entire contents of the skillet over the pork, add the remaining 3½ cups of chicken stock, the chopped celery leaves and the parsley and bring the casserole to a boil. Reduce the heat to low and simmer, partially covered, for 2 hours, or until the pork is tender and shows no resistance when pierced with the point of a small sharp knife.

With a large spoon, skim as much fat as possible from the surface of the stew. Taste for seasoning and serve the backbone stew at once, directly from the casserole or from a heated bowl.

Pot-roasted Rabbit

To serve 4 to 6

4 slices bacon
A 2½- to 3-pound rabbit,
    thoroughly defrosted if frozen,
    and cut into 8 serving pieces
1 teaspoon salt
½ teaspoon freshly ground black
    pepper
1 cup flour
4 tablespoons butter
½ cup finely chopped onions
¼ cup finely chopped green pepper
¼ pound firm fresh mushrooms,

trimmed, wiped with a dampened
    cloth and cut lengthwise,
    including the stems, into ¼-
    inch-thick slices
1 teaspoon finely chopped garlic
1 cup water
1 teaspoon Worcestershire sauce
½ teaspoon dry mustard
½ teaspoon sugar
1 tablespoon finely chopped fresh
    parsley, preferably the flat-leaf
    Italian variety

In a heavy 12-inch skillet, fry the bacon over moderate heat, turning the slices frequently with tongs until they are crisp and brown and have rendered all their fat. Transfer the bacon to paper towels to drain; crumble it into small bits and reserve them.

Pat the pieces of rabbit completely dry with paper towels and season them on all sides with the salt and black pepper. Roll one piece at a time in the flour to coat it lightly, and vigorously shake off the excess flour. Then brown the rabbit in the bacon fat remaining in the skillet, starting the pieces skin side down and turning them frequently with tongs. Regulate the heat so that the rabbit colors richly and evenly without burning. As they brown, transfer the pieces of rabbit to a plate.

Add the butter to the fat remaining in the skillet and melt it over moderate heat. When the foam begins to subside, drop in the onions, green pepper, mushrooms and garlic. Stirring frequently, cook for about 5 minutes, or until the vegetables are soft but not brown. Add the water, Worcestershire sauce, mustard and sugar, and bring to a boil over high heat, meanwhile scraping in the brown particles that cling to the bottom and sides of the skillet.

Return the rabbit and the liquid that has accumulated around it to the skillet and baste it well with the vegetable mixture. Reduce the heat to low and simmer, partially covered, for about 1 hour, or until the rabbit is tender and shows no resistance when pierced deeply with the point of a small sharp knife. Taste for seasoning.

To serve, arrange the pot-roasted rabbit attractively on a deep heated platter and ladle the sauce and vegetables over it. Garnish the top with the reserved bacon bits and the parsley.

Veal Stew

To serve 8 to 10

4 pounds lean boneless veal shoulder, trimmed of excess fat and cut into 1½-inch cubes
2 teaspoons salt
¼ teaspoon freshly ground black pepper
½ cup flour
4 tablespoons butter
¼ to ½ cup vegetable oil
2 cups finely chopped onions
½ cup finely chopped green pepper
1 tablespoon finely chopped garlic
2 cups chicken stock, fresh or canned

½ pound lean cooked smoked ham, sliced ½ inch thick and cut into ½-inch cubes
2 one-pound cans tomatoes, drained and coarsely chopped, with all their liquid reserved
3 medium-sized yams (1 pound), peeled and cut into 1-inch chunks
4 fresh parsley sprigs and 1 large bay leaf, tied together
¼ teaspoon ground hot red pepper (cayenne)
1 pound fresh okra, washed, trimmed and cut crosswise into 1-inch-thick rounds

Pat the cubes of veal dry with paper towels and season them on all sides with 1 teaspoon of the salt and the black pepper. Roll one piece at a time in the flour to coat it lightly and shake off the excess flour.

In a heavy 12-inch skillet, melt the butter with ¼ cup of oil over moderate heat. When the foam begins to subside, add about half the veal and brown it, turning the pieces frequently with tongs and regulating the heat so that they color richly and evenly without burning. When the first batch of veal is browned, transfer it to a heavy 8-quart casserole and brown the remaining pieces in the same fashion, adding up to ¼ cup more oil to the skillet if necessary.

Pour off all but a thin film of fat from the skillet and add the onions, green pepper and garlic. Stirring frequently, cook over moderate heat for about 5 minutes, or until the vegetables are soft but not brown. Transfer the vegetables to the casserole with the veal, pour the chicken stock into the skillet and bring it to a boil over high heat, meanwhile scraping in any brown particles that cling to the bottom and sides of the pan. Pour the stock mixture over the veal.

Stir the ham, tomatoes, yams, parsley sprigs and bay leaf, the red pepper and the remaining teaspoon of salt into the veal mixture and bring to a boil over high heat. Reduce the heat to low, cover the casserole partially, and simmer for 1½ hours. Stir in the okra and simmer, partially covered, for about 30 minutes longer, until the veal is tender and shows no resistance when pierced with the point of a small sharp knife.

Pick out and discard the parsley sprigs and bay leaf, and taste the stew for seasoning. Serve at once, directly from the casserole or from a large heated bowl.

Veal Rolls and Olives

To serve 4 or 8

8 tablespoons butter
1 cup soft fresh crumbs made from French- or Italian-type white bread, pulverized in a blender
½ cup finely chopped onions
½ pound lean cooked smoked ham, sliced ⅛ inch thick and finely chopped
1 hard-cooked egg, finely chopped
¼ teaspoon crumbled dried thyme
⅛ teaspoon ground hot red pepper

(cayenne)
½ teaspoon salt
Eight 6-by-4-inch veal scallops (about 4 ounces each), cut about ⅜ inch thick and pounded ¼ inch thick
¼ cup flour
2 tablespoons vegetable oil
1 cup chicken stock, fresh or canned
½ cup pitted green olives, coarsely chopped

In a heavy 12-inch skillet, melt 4 tablespoons of the butter over moderate heat. When the foam begins to subside, add the bread crumbs and stir until they are crisp and golden brown. With a slotted spoon, transfer the crumbs to a bowl.

Melt 2 tablespoons of the remaining butter in the same skillet and, when the foam subsides, drop in the onions. Stirring frequently, cook over moderate heat for about 5 minutes, or until they are soft and translucent but not brown. With a rubber spatula, scrape the entire contents of the skillet over the bread crumbs. Add the ham, egg, thyme, red pepper and salt, and toss all the stuffing ingredients together gently but thoroughly. Set the skillet aside.

Pat the veal scallops dry with paper towels. To make each veal roll, spread about ¼ cup of the stuffing mixture on each scallop in a band about 1 inch from one narrow end of the scallop. Fold the end over the stuffing and roll up the scallop into a tight cylinder. Tie the roll securely in shape with two or three short lengths of kitchen cord and turn it about in the flour to coat the surface lightly.

Place the reserved skillet over moderate heat and in it melt the remaining 2 tablespoons of butter with the oil. Add the veal rolls and brown them on all sides, turning them with tongs or a spatula and regulating the heat so that they color richly and evenly without burning. As they brown, transfer the veal rolls to a plate.

Pour the chicken stock into the fat remaining in the skillet and bring to a boil over high heat, meanwhile scraping in the brown particles that cling to the bottom and sides of the pan. Stir in the olives, then return the veal rolls and the liquid that has accumulated around them to the skillet. Cover tightly, reduce the heat to low and simmer for about 1 hour, or until the veal is tender and shows no resistance when pierced deeply with the point of a small sharp knife.

With a slotted spatula, transfer the veal rolls to a heated platter. Taste the olive sauce for seasoning, pour it over the veal and serve at once.

Grillades and Grits
BRAISED VEAL STEAKS WITH HOMINY GRITS

To serve 4

Four 5- to 6-ounce boneless veal
   round steaks, sliced ½ inch thick
   and trimmed of excess fat
2 teaspoons salt
¼ teaspoon freshly ground black
   pepper
½ cup flour
3 tablespoons lard
4 tablespoons butter
2 large onions, peeled and coarsely
   chopped
1½ cups coarsely chopped green
   peppers

½ cup coarsely chopped celery
1 tablespoon finely chopped garlic
2 cups chicken stock, fresh or
   canned
1½ cups coarsely chopped drained
   canned tomatoes
1 medium-sized bay leaf
1 tablespoon cornstarch combined
   with 1 tablespoon cold water
5 cups water
1 cup regular yellow or white
   hominy grits, not the quick-
   cooking variety

Pat the veal steaks completely dry with paper towels and season them with 1 teaspoon of the salt and the black pepper. One at a time, dip the steaks in the flour to coat them evenly. Then shake off the excess flour.

In a heavy 12-inch skillet, melt the lard over moderate heat until it is very hot but not smoking. Brown the veal steaks, two at a time, turning them with tongs and regulating the heat so that they color richly on both sides without burning. As they brown, transfer the steak to a plate.

Pour off the fat remaining in the skillet, add the butter, and melt it over moderate heat. When the foam begins to subside, add the onions, green peppers, celery and garlic and, stirring frequently, cook for about 5 minutes, or until the vegetables are soft but not brown. Stir in the stock, tomatoes and bay leaf, and bring to a boil over high heat. Reduce the heat to low, partially cover the skillet, and simmer for 20 minutes.

Return the steaks and the liquid that has accumulated around them to the skillet and turn to coat them with the vegetable mixture. Simmer partially covered for about 1 hour, or until the veal is tender and shows no resistance when pierced with the point of a small sharp knife. Pour the cornstarch-and-water mixture over the simmering veal and stir for 2 or 3 minutes, until the gravy thickens slightly. Taste for seasoning.

About half an hour before the veal is done, bring the water and the remaining teaspoon of salt to a boil in a heavy 1½- to 2-quart saucepan. Pour in the hominy grits slowly enough so that the boiling continues at a rapid rate, stirring all the while with a wooden spoon to keep the mixture smooth. Reduce the heat to low and, stirring occasionally, simmer the grits tightly covered for 30 minutes.

Mound the grits on heated individual plates or a deep platter and place the veal steaks on the top. Pour the gravy over the grits and steaks and serve at once. (If allowed to cool, the grits will be undesirably firm.)

Mustard Greens and Turnips

To serve 4

½ pound fresh mustard greens
3 medium-sized turnips (about
 ¾ pound), scraped, sliced into
 ¼-inch-thick rounds and cut into
 ¼-inch dice

1 tablespoon sugar
1 teaspoon salt
6 tablespoons vegetable oil
1½ cups finely chopped onion
⅛ teaspoon ground hot red pepper
 (cayenne)

Wash the mustard greens under cold running water. With a small sharp knife, trim off any bruised or blemished spots and strip the leaves away from their stems.

Drop the mustard greens into a small saucepan, add enough water to cover them, and bring to a boil over high heat. Cover the pan tightly, reduce the heat to low and simmer 5 to 10 minutes, or until the greens are wilted and soft. Drain them in a sieve or colander and set aside.

Meanwhile, combine the turnips, sugar and salt in a separate small saucepan and pour in enough water to cover them by at least 1 inch. Bring to a boil over high heat, reduce the heat to low and simmer, partially covered, for about 10 minutes, or until the turnips are tender but still intact. Drain the turnips in a sieve or colander and reserve them.

In a heavy 10- to 12-inch skillet, heat the oil over moderate heat until a light haze forms above it. Drop in the onions and, stirring frequently, cook for about 5 minutes, or until they are soft and translucent but not brown. Add the reserved mustard greens and turnips and the cayenne and, stirring from time to time, simmer over low heat until the greens and turnips are heated through.

Taste for seasoning and serve at once from a heated bowl.

Red Beans and Rice

To serve 4 to 6

6 cups water
1 pound dried small red beans *(see Glossary, page 150)* or 1 pound dried red kidney beans
4 tablespoons butter
1 cup finely chopped scallions, including 3 inches of the green tops

½ cup finely chopped onions
1 teaspoon finely chopped garlic
2 one-pound smoked ham hocks
1 teaspoon salt
½ teaspoon freshly ground black pepper
6 to 8 cups freshly cooked long-grain rice

In a heavy 3- to 4-quart saucepan, bring the water to a boil over high heat. Drop in the beans and boil briskly, uncovered, for 2 minutes. Then turn off the heat and let the beans soak for 1 hour. Drain the beans in a sieve set over a large bowl; measure the soaking liquid and, if necessary, add more water to make 4 cups. Set the beans and liquid aside.

Melt the butter in a heavy 4- to 5-quart casserole set over moderate heat. When the foam begins to subside, add ½ cup of the scallions, the onions and the garlic and, stirring frequently, cook for about 5 minutes, or until they are soft and translucent but not brown.

Stir in the beans and their liquid, the ham hocks, salt and pepper. Bring the mixture to a boil over high heat, reduce the heat to low and simmer partially covered for about 3 hours, or until the beans are very soft. Check the pot from time to time and, if the beans seem dry, add up to 1 cup more water, a few tablespoonfuls at a time. During the last 30 minutes or so of cooking, stir frequently and mash the softest beans against the sides of the pan to form a thick sauce for the remaining beans.

With tongs or a slotted spoon, transfer the ham hocks to a plate. Cut the meat away from the bones and remove and discard the skin, fat and gristle. Cut the meat into ¼-inch dice and return it to the beans.

Taste the red beans for seasoning and serve at once, directly from the casserole or from a large heated tureen. Place the rice and the remaining ½ cup of scallions in separate bowls and present them with the beans.

NOTE: In Louisiana, red beans and rice are traditionally made with a leftover ham bone, and you may substitute a ham bone for the ham hocks in this recipe. Without trimming off the meat, cut the bone into 2- or 3-inch pieces with a hacksaw, so that the marrow inside the pieces will melt and flavor the beans. Add the pieces of bone to the soaked bean mixture and pour in enough additional water to cover them completely. When the beans are cooked, remove the bones from the pot, trim off and dice the meat, and return it to the beans. Discard the bones.

Stewed Lima Beans

To serve 6

2 quarts water
2 cups (1 pound) dried large Lima
 beans
A ¾-pound smoked ham hock
1 large onion, peeled, plus 1 large
 onion, peeled and sliced
 lengthwise into ¼-inch-thick
 slices
1 medium-sized bay leaf

½ pound lean salt pork with rind
 removed, cut into ¼-inch-thick
 slices
Salt (optional)
Freshly ground black pepper
 (optional)
½ cup finely chopped scallions,
 including 3 inches of the green
 tops

In a heavy 6- to 8-quart casserole, bring the water to a boil over high heat. Drop in the Lima beans and boil briskly for 2 minutes, then remove the casserole from the heat and let the beans soak for 1 hour. Add the ham hock, the whole onion and the bay leaf and return the water to a boil over high heat. Reduce the heat to low and simmer, partially covered, for about 1 hour, or until the Lima beans are tender but still intact. Check the casserole from time to time and add more boiling water if the liquid seems to be cooking away too rapidly.

Transfer the ham hock to a platter, and remove and discard the whole onion and bay leaf. Drain the beans through a large sieve set over a bowl and reserve the beans and 2 cups of the cooking liquid. When the ham is cool enough to handle, cut off the skin and fat with a small sharp knife and remove the meat from the bones. Discard the skin, fat and bones and cut the meat into ¼-inch pieces.

Fry the salt pork slices in a heavy 3- to 4-quart casserole set over moderate heat, turning them frequently with tongs until they are crisp and brown and have rendered all their fat. Transfer the pork to paper towels to drain and pour off all but about 2 tablespoons of the fat. Add the sliced onion to the casserole and, stirring frequently, cook for about 5 minutes, or until the onion is soft and translucent but not brown. Stir in the reserved beans, the 2 cups of bean liquid, the ham meat and the salt-pork slices and bring to a boil over high heat. Taste for seasoning and add salt and freshly ground black pepper if you wish. Sprinkle the top with the chopped scallions and serve at once, directly from the casserole.

Spiced Stewed Okra

To serve 6

1½ pounds fresh okra
3 large firm ripe tomatoes
½ pound sliced bacon, cut
crosswise into halves
1½ cups coarsely chopped onions

1 cup coarsely chopped green
peppers
3 dried hot red chilies, each about
2 inches long, washed, stemmed,
seeded and coarsely crumbled
(*caution: see note, page 6*)
1 teaspoon salt

Wash the okra under cold running water and, with a small sharp knife, scrape the skin lightly to remove any surface fuzz. Cut off the stems and slice each pod crosswise into ½-inch rounds.

Drop the tomatoes into boiling water and remove them after 15 seconds. Run them under cold water and, with a small sharp knife, peel them, cut out the stems, then slice the tomatoes in half crosswise. Squeeze the halves gently to remove the seeds and juice, and chop the pulp coarsely.

Fry the bacon in a heavy 12-inch skillet set over moderate heat, turning the slices frequently with tongs until they are crisp and brown and have rendered all their fat. Transfer the bacon to paper towels to drain.

Pour off all but about ¼ cup of the fat remaining in the skillet and add the onions and green peppers. Stirring frequently, cook over moderate heat for 5 minutes, or until the vegetables are soft but not brown.

Add the okra and, still stirring from time to time, cook uncovered for about 15 minutes. When the okra is tender, add the tomatoes, chilies and salt, reduce the heat to low, and simmer, tightly covered, for 10 minutes.

Taste for seasoning, then mound the okra in a heated serving bowl and sprinkle the bacon slices on top. Serve at once.

Sherry-baked Bananas

To serve 4

¼ cup dry sherry
¼ cup dark brown sugar
3 tablespoons apricot jam or apricot
preserves
2 tablespoons butter, melted and

cooled
2 tablespoons strained fresh lemon
juice
4 large ripe bananas, peeled and cut
lengthwise into halves

Preheat the oven to 350°. Combine the sherry, brown sugar, apricot jam or preserves, melted butter and lemon juice in a small bowl and stir until the ingredients are well blended. Arrange the banana halves, cut side down and in one layer, in a shallow, unbuttered baking dish large enough to hold them snugly. Spread the sherry mixture evenly over the bananas, then bake in the middle of the oven for 30 minutes, or until the bananas are tender and show no resistance when pierced deeply with the point of a small sharp knife. Serve at once, directly from the baking dish.

Dirty Rice

To serve 6 to 8

½ pound chicken gizzards, thoroughly defrosted if frozen, trimmed of excess fat and coarsely chopped

½ pound chicken livers, thoroughly defrosted if frozen, and coarsely chopped

2 medium-sized onions, peeled and coarsely chopped

1 large green pepper, stemmed, seeded, deribbed and coarsely chopped

½ cup coarsely chopped celery

2 tablespoons olive oil

1½ teaspoons salt

½ teaspoon freshly ground black pepper

1 cup uncooked long-grain white rice, not the converted variety

2 cups water

½ cup finely chopped fresh parsley

The term dirty rice may be a jocular reference to the appearance of the finished dish, since the bits of chicken gizzard and liver that are tossed with the rice give it a brown, or "dirty," look.

Put the chicken gizzards, chicken livers, onions, green pepper and celery through the finest blade of a food grinder. In a heavy 4- to 5-quart casserole, heat the olive oil over moderate heat until a light haze forms above it. Add the ground chicken mixture, stir in the salt and black pepper, and reduce the heat to low. Stirring occasionally, cook uncovered for about 1 hour, or until the bits of chicken are richly browned.

Meanwhile, place the rice in a heavy 1-quart pot, stir in the water and bring to a boil over high heat. Reduce the heat to low, cover tightly, and simmer for 20 to 25 minutes, or until the rice has absorbed all the liquid in the pan and the grains are tender. Remove the pan from the heat and let the rice rest, still tightly covered, for 10 minutes or so.

When the chicken mixture has cooked its allotted time, fluff the rice with a fork and add it to the casserole. With the fork, toss the rice and the chicken mixture together gently but thoroughly.

Taste for seasoning and stir in the parsley. Mound the dirty rice on a heated platter or in a heated serving bowl and serve at once.

Green Rice

To serve 4 to 6

4 tablespoons butter	1 cup coarsely chopped scallions,
1 cup uncooked long-grain white	including 3 inches of the green
rice	tops
2 cups boiling water	1 cup coarsely chopped fresh
1 teaspoon salt	parsley, preferably the flat-leaf
¼ teaspoon ground white pepper	Italian variety

In a heavy 2- to 3-quart saucepan, melt 2 tablespoons of the butter over moderate heat. When the foam begins to subside, add the rice and stir for 2 or 3 minutes to coat the grains with butter. Do not let the rice brown. Add the water, salt and pepper and, still stirring, bring to a boil over high heat. Cover the pan tightly and reduce the heat to its lowest point. Simmer undisturbed for 20 minutes, or until all the liquid has been absorbed by the rice and the grains are tender but not too soft.

Meanwhile, melt the remaining 2 tablespoons of butter in a heavy 8- to 10-inch skillet set over moderate heat. Drop in the scallions and parsley, and stir for 2 or 3 minutes, until they are soft and wilted. Remove the pan from the heat. When the rice has cooked its allotted time, add the scallions and parsley, and fluff them together with a fork. Taste for seasoning and serve at once from a heated bowl.

Jerusalem-Artichoke Purée

To serve 4 to 6

	3 teaspoons salt
3 tablespoons strained fresh lemon	4 tablespoons butter, cut into
juice	½-inch bits
5 pounds Jerusalem artichokes	½ teaspoon ground white pepper

Combine the lemon juice and about 3 quarts of cold water in a deep pot. Then, with a small sharp knife, peel the Jerusalem artichokes, dropping them into the lemon-water mixture to prevent discoloring as you proceed.

Drain the artichokes, transfer them to a heavy 4- to 5-quart saucepan, and add 2 teaspoons of the salt and enough fresh water to cover them by 1 inch. Bring to a boil over high heat, reduce the heat to low and partially cover the pan. Simmer for 20 minutes, or until one of the artichokes can be mashed against the side of the pan with the back of a large spoon.

Pour off the cooking liquid and purée the artichokes through a potato ricer set over a deep bowl. Then return them to the saucepan and, stirring constantly, cook over low heat until all of the liquid in the pan has evaporated. Beat in the butter and, when the bits have melted completely, add the remaining teaspoon of salt and the white pepper.

Taste for seasoning, mound the Jerusalem-artichoke purée in a heated bowl and serve at once.

Shrimp-stuffed Artichokes

To serve 4

4 large artichokes, each 4 to 5 inches
    in diameter at the base
1 lemon, cut in half crosswise
Salt
1 pound uncooked shrimp
½ pound plus 4 tablespoons
    butter, cut into ½-inch bits
6 cups soft fresh crumbs made from
    French- or Italian-type white
    bread, pulverized in a blender or
    finely shredded with a fork

1 cup finely chopped onions
4 teaspoons finely chopped garlic
2 cups freshly grated imported
    Romano or Parmesan cheese
½ cup finely chopped fresh
    parsley, preferably the flat-leaf
    Italian variety
2 teaspoons finely grated fresh
    lemon peel
½ cup Creole vinaigrette sauce
    (page 103)

With a small sharp knife, trim the bases of the artichokes flush and flat. Bend and snap off the small bottom leaves and any bruised outer leaves. Lay each artichoke on its side and slice about 1 inch off the top. With scissors, trim ¼ inch off the points of the rest of the leaves. To prevent discoloring, rub all the cut edges with lemon as you proceed.

In a 10- to 12-quart enameled pot, bring 5 quarts of water and 2 tablespoons of salt to a boil over high heat. Drop in the artichokes and one lemon half and return the water to a boil. Cook briskly, uncovered, for 15 to 20 minutes, or until the bases of the artichokes show no resistance when pierced with the point of a small sharp knife.

With tongs, invert the artichokes in a colander to drain. Discard the lemon and all but about 1 inch of the cooking liquid. Set the pot aside.

Meanwhile, shell the shrimp. Make a shallow incision down their backs with a small sharp knife and lift out the intestinal vein with the point of the knife. Wash the shrimp briefly in a colander set under cold running water. Then drop them into enough lightly salted boiling water to immerse the shrimp completely. Cook uncovered for 3 to 5 minutes, until they are pink and firm to the touch. Drain the shrimp and pat them dry with paper towels. Reserve four of the shrimp for garnish and chop the rest into fine bits. Set the shrimp aside.

Melt ½ pound of the butter bits in a heavy 12-inch skillet set over moderate heat, stirring so that the butter melts without browning. When the foam begins to subside, add the bread crumbs and stir over moderate heat until the crumbs are crisp and golden. With a rubber spatula, scrape the contents of the skillet into a bowl and set it aside.

In the same skillet, melt the remaining 4 tablespoons of butter bits over moderate heat. When the foam subsides, add the onions and garlic, and stir for about 5 minutes, until they are soft and translucent but not brown. Scrape the onion mixture over the bread crumbs, add the reserved shrimp, grated cheese, parsley and lemon peel, and toss the ingredients together gently but thoroughly with a spoon. Taste for seasoning.

Divide the shrimp mixture into four equal portions and stuff each artichoke in the following fashion: Starting near the base, gently ease the top of one leaf away from the artichoke and spoon about a teaspoonful of the shrimp mixture into the opening. Push the shrimp mixture down between the leaf and the artichoke, then press the leaf back into place.

Repeat until all of the large green outer leaves have been stuffed, then stand the artichoke upright on a large piece of heavy-duty aluminum foil. Fold the foil tightly up and around the artichoke, and twist the ends securely together at the top. To keep the stuffing in place, tie a short length of kitchen cord around the widest part of the foil package. Set aside. Stuff and wrap the remaining artichokes in the same way.

Stand the artichokes upright in the reserved pot and bring the liquid to a boil over high heat. Cover tightly and steam the artichokes for 20 minutes. With tongs, transfer the artichokes to a cutting board and remove the strings and foil. Arrange the artichokes attractively on a heated platter or four individual serving plates, and place one of the reserved whole shrimp on top of each one. Serve the Creole vinaigrette sauce separately as an accompaniment to the inner leaves and bottom of the artichokes.

Glazed Mirliton

To serve 6 to 8

4 pounds mirliton squash (see
   Glossary, page 150)
3 tablespoons strained fresh lemon
   juice
1 cup light brown sugar
½ teaspoon ground cinnamon
¼ teaspoon ground allspice

¼ teaspoon ground ginger
¼ teaspoon ground nutmeg,
   preferably freshly grated
⅛ teaspoon ground cloves
½ teaspoon salt
4 tablespoons butter, cut into
   ¼-inch bits

Preheat the oven to 350°. With a small sharp knife, peel the mirlitons and cut them lengthwise in half. Remove and discard the seeds, and slice each squash lengthwise into strips about ⅓ inch thick. As you proceed, drop the squash into a deep bowl. Add the lemon juice and turn the slices about with a spoon to moisten them evenly.

Combine the brown sugar, cinnamon, allspice, ginger, nutmeg, cloves and salt in a bowl and mix well. Sprinkle the mixture over the squash and toss them together gently but thoroughly.

Transfer the entire contents of the bowl to an ungreased 13-by-9-by-2-inch baking dish and scatter the butter bits over the top. Bake in the middle of the oven for 45 minutes, stirring occasionally to coat the squash slices with the syrupy glaze.

Increase the oven temperature to 400° and bake for 20 to 30 minutes longer, or until the squash are tender and the glaze is thick and shiny. Serve the mirliton at once, directly from the baking dish.

Shrimp-stuffed Mirliton

To serve 8

4 eight-ounce mirliton squash *(see Glossary, page 150)*
½ pound uncooked shrimp
½ pound lean cooked smoked ham, coarsely chopped
1 medium-sized onion, peeled and coarsely chopped
2 medium-sized garlic cloves, peeled and coarsely chopped
¼ cup finely chopped fresh parsley, preferably the flat-leaf

Italian variety
¼ teaspoon ground thyme
½ teaspoon ground hot red pepper (cayenne)
½ teaspoon salt
1 tablespoon butter, softened, plus 11 tablespoons butter, cut into ½-inch bits
1 cup soft fresh crumbs made from French- or Italian-type white bread, pulverized in a blender or finely shredded with a fork

Drop the mirlitons into enough boiling water to immerse them completely. Cook briskly, uncovered, for about 45 minutes, or until they show no resistance when pierced with the point of a small sharp knife.

Meanwhile, shell the shrimp. Devein them by making a shallow incision down their backs with a small sharp knife and lifting out the intestinal vein with the point of the knife. Wash the shrimp briefly in a colander set under cold running water, then drop them into enough boiling salted water to cover them completely. Cook briskly, uncovered, for 3 to 5 minutes, or until the shrimp are pink and firm to the touch. Drain the shrimp and pat them completely dry with fresh towels. Put the shrimp, ham, onion and garlic through the medium blade of a food grinder, stir in the parsley, thyme, red pepper and salt, and set aside.

Preheat the oven to 375°. With a pastry brush, spread the tablespoon of softened butter over the bottom and sides of a shallow baking dish large enough to hold the squash snugly in one layer.

Drain the mirlitons and, when they are cool enough to handle, cut them lengthwise into halves. Remove the seeds, and hollow out each half with a spoon to make boatlike shells about ¼ inch thick. Invert the shells on paper towels to drain. Purée the pulp through a food mill set over a bowl or drop the pulp into a bowl and, with the back of a fork, mash it to a purée. Transfer the pulp to a heavy ungreased 12-inch skillet and, stirring constantly, cook over moderate heat until all of the liquid in the pan evaporates. Add 8 tablespoons of the butter bits to the purée and, when it melts, stir in the ground shrimp mixture. Taste for seasoning.

Spoon the shrimp-and-squash stuffing into the reserved mirliton shells, dividing it equally among them and mounding the tops slightly. Sprinkle the bread crumbs and the remaining 3 tablespoons of butter bits over the mirlitons. Arrange the shells in the buttered dish and bake in the middle of the oven for 30 minutes, or until the tops are brown. Serve at once.

Leeks Vinaigrette

To serve 4 as a salad

8 firm fresh leeks, each 1 to 1½ inches in diameter	½ cup Creole vinaigrette sauce *(below)*

With a sharp knife, cut off the roots of the leeks and strip away any withered leaves. Line up the leeks in a row and cut off enough of their green tops to make each leek 6 or 7 inches long. Then slit the green parts in half lengthwise, stopping within about ½ inch of the root ends. Carefully spread the leaves apart and wash the leeks under cold running water to rid them of all sand.

Lay the leeks in one or two layers in a heavy stainless-steel or enameled skillet or casserole just large enough to hold them flat. Pour in enough cold water to cover them by about 1 inch and bring to a boil over high heat. Reduce the heat to low, cover the pan partially, and simmer for 10 minutes, or until the leeks show only the slightest resistance when their bases are pierced with a fork.

With tongs or a slotted spoon, transfer the leeks to a double thickness of paper towels and let them drain for a minute or two. Arrange the leeks attractively in a serving dish or deep platter and pour the Creole vinaigrette sauce over them. Cool to room temperature, then refrigerate the leeks for at least 1 hour to chill them thoroughly before serving.

Creole Vinaigrette Sauce

To make about ½ cup

2 tablespoons tarragon vinegar	¼ teaspoon ground hot red pepper (cayenne)
1 teaspoon paprika	
½ teaspoon Creole mustard *(see Glossary, page 150)*	½ teaspoon salt
	6 to 8 tablespoons olive oil

Combine the vinegar, paprika, mustard, red pepper and salt in a deep bowl and beat vigorously with a wire whisk to dissolve the salt. Whisking constantly, dribble in the oil a few drops at a time until no more oil is absorbed. When the sauce is thick and smooth, taste for seasoning.

Creole vinaigrette may be served immediately or, if you prefer, cover the bowl tightly with foil or plastic wrap, and set the sauce aside at room temperature until you are ready to use it.

Chicken-stuffed Baked Tomatoes

To serve 4

½ pound chicken breast
1 teaspoon salt
Freshly ground black pepper
¼ pound lean, boneless smoked
    ham, cut into chunks
4 large firm ripe tomatoes, each
    about 3 inches in diameter
1 tablespoon butter, softened, plus
    4 tablespoons butter, cut into
    ¼-inch bits
1 cup finely chopped onions

1 tablespoon finely chopped fresh
    parsley, preferably the flat-leaf
    Italian variety
1 medium-sized bay leaf, finely
    crumbled
¼ teaspoon crumbled dried thyme
¼ teaspoon ground hot red pepper
    (cayenne)
½ cup plus 2 tablespoons soft
    fresh crumbs made from French-
    or Italian-type white bread,
    pulverized in a blender

Combine the chicken breast, ½ teaspoon of the salt and a few grindings of black pepper in a small saucepan and pour in enough water to cover the chicken completely. Bring to a boil over high heat, reduce the heat to low and simmer partially covered for about 10 minutes, or until the chicken feels firm when prodded gently with a finger. Transfer the chicken breast to a plate to drain and, when it is cool enough to handle, remove the skin. With your fingers or a small sharp knife, pull or cut the meat from the bones. Discard the skin and bones and cut the meat into small chunks. Then put the chicken meat and the ham through the finest blade of a food grinder. (There should be 1½ to 2 cups of ground meat.)

Cut a ¼-inch-thick slice off the top of each tomato and, with a small spoon, scoop out the pulp to create a shell about ¼ inch thick. Invert the tomato shells on paper towels to drain, chop the pulp coarsely, and reserve it in a small bowl.

Preheat the oven to 350°. With a pastry brush, spread the tablespoon of softened butter over the bottom and sides of a shallow baking dish large enough to hold the tomatoes snugly in one layer. Set the dish aside.

In a heavy 10- to 12-inch skillet, melt 2 tablespoons of the butter bits over moderate heat. When the foam begins to subside, add the onions and, stirring frequently, cook for about 5 minutes, or until they are soft and translucent but not brown. Add the reserved tomato pulp, the parsley, bay leaf, thyme, red pepper, the remaining ½ teaspoon of salt and a few grindings of black pepper. Stirring frequently, cook briskly until most of the liquid in the pan has evaporated and the mixture is thick enough to hold its shape almost solidly in a spoon. Add ½ cup of the bread crumbs and the reserved ground chicken and ham, and mix well. Taste the stuffing for seasoning.

Spoon the stuffing into the tomato shells, dividing it equally among them and mounding the centers slightly. Arrange the tomatoes side by side in the buttered dish and sprinkle the tops with the remaining 2 tablespoons of bread crumbs and 2 tablespoons of butter bits.

Bake in the middle of the oven for 45 minutes, or until the tomato shells are tender when pierced with the point of a small sharp knife and the stuffing is golden brown. Serve at once, directly from the baking dish or attractively arranged on a heated platter.

Creole Tomatoes

To serve 8

1 tablespoon butter, softened, plus 4 tablespoons butter, plus 2 tablespoons butter, cut into ¼-inch bits	Italian variety
½ cup finely chopped onions	4 large firm ripe tomatoes, washed, stemmed and sliced crosswise in half
½ cup finely chopped green pepper	1½ teaspoons salt
1½ teaspoons finely chopped garlic	Freshly ground black pepper
1 tablespoon finely chopped fresh parsley, preferably the flat-leaf	2 tablespoons flour
	1 cup light cream
	⅛ teaspoon Tabasco sauce

Preheat the oven to 350°. With a pastry brush, spread the tablespoon of softened butter evenly over the bottom and sides of a 13-by-9-by-2-inch baking dish. Set the dish aside.

In a heavy 8- to 10-inch skillet, melt 2 tablespoons of butter over moderate heat. When the foam subsides, add the onions, green pepper and garlic and, stirring frequently, cook for 5 minutes, until the vegetables are soft but not brown. Remove the pan from the heat and stir in the parsley.

Arrange the tomato halves, cut side up, in one layer in the buttered dish and sprinkle them with 1 teaspoon of the salt and a few grindings of black pepper. Spoon the onion mixture over the tomatoes, dividing it evenly among them, and scatter the 2 tablespoons of butter bits over the tops. Bake in the middle of the oven for 30 minutes, or until the tomatoes are tender but not limp.

Meanwhile, prepare the sauce in the following manner: Melt the remaining 2 tablespoons of butter in a small, heavy saucepan set over moderate heat. Add the flour and mix well.

Stirring constantly with a wire whisk, pour in the cream in a slow, thin stream and cook over high heat until the sauce comes to a boil, thickens lightly and is smooth. Reduce the heat to low and simmer for 2 or 3 minutes to remove the raw taste of the flour. Stir in the remaining ½ teaspoon of salt and the Tabasco, and taste the sauce for seasoning.

With a metal spatula transfer the baked Creole tomatoes to a heated platter. Pour the sauce over the tomatoes, masking each of them completely, and serve at once.

Maquechou
INDIAN-STYLE STEWED CORN AND TOMATOES

To serve 4 to 6

¼ cup bacon drippings
2 medium-sized onions, peeled and coarsely chopped
1 teaspoon finely chopped garlic
4 cups fresh corn kernels, cut from 5 or 6 large ears of corn, or substitute 4 cups frozen corn kernels, thoroughly defrosted
1 medium-sized green pepper, stemmed, quartered, seeded, deribbed and coarsely chopped
A 1-pound 12-ounce can whole tomatoes, drained and coarsely chopped, with all the liquid reserved
1 cup water
½ teaspoon ground hot red pepper (cayenne)
1½ teaspoons salt

In a heavy 4- to 5-quart casserole, melt the bacon drippings over moderate heat. Add the onions and garlic and, stirring frequently, cook for about 5 minutes, or until the onions are soft and translucent but not brown. Stir in the corn, green pepper, tomatoes and tomato liquid, water, red pepper and salt, and bring to a boil over high heat. Reduce the heat to low, cover the casserole partially, and simmer for about 10 minutes, or until the corn is tender. Taste for seasoning and serve at once, directly from the casserole or from a heated bowl.

Yams and Sausage
To serve 6

1 tablespoon butter, softened, plus 4 tablespoons butter
2 pounds yams
1½ cups soft fresh crumbs made from French- or Italian-type white bread, pulverized in a blender
½ pound fresh pork sausage meat, the breakfast-sausage variety
½ cup finely chopped onions
½ cup finely chopped celery
½ teaspoon poultry seasoning
¼ teaspoon salt
¼ teaspoon freshly ground black pepper

Preheat the oven to 375°. With a pastry brush, spread the tablespoon of softened butter evenly over the bottom and sides of a 1½-quart baking dish. Set the dish aside.

Drop the yams into enough boiling water to cover them completely and cook briskly, uncovered, for about 20 minutes, or until the yams are tender and show no resistance when pierced deeply with the point of a small sharp knife. Drain the yams and peel them with a small sharp knife. Purée the yams through a potato ricer set over a bowl, or place them in a bowl and mash them to a smooth purée with the back of a fork.

In a heavy 10- to 12-inch skillet, melt the remaining 4 tablespoons of butter over moderate heat. Drop in the bread crumbs and, stirring frequently, fry until they are crisp and brown. With a slotted spoon, transfer the toasted bread crumbs to a bowl. Add the sausage meat to the fat remaining in the skillet and cook over moderate heat, mashing the meat frequently to break up any lumps that develop, until no trace of pink shows. With the slotted spoon, add the meat to the bowl of bread crumbs.

Pour off all but a thin film of fat from the skillet and add the onions and celery. Stirring from time to time, cook over moderate heat for about 5 minutes, or until the vegetables are soft but not brown. Using a rubber spatula, scrape the contents of the skillet over the sausage and crumbs.

Add the puréed yams, poultry seasoning, salt and pepper, and stir until all the ingredients are well blended. Taste for seasoning. Transfer the mixture to the buttered dish, spreading it evenly and smoothing the top with the spatula. Bake in the middle of the oven for about 25 minutes, or until the top is golden brown and crusty. Serve the yams and sausage at once, directly from the baking dish.

Green Peas à la française

To serve 8

1 small firm head of iceberg lettuce (about ½ pound)	4 cups shelled fresh green peas (about 4 pounds before shelling)
4 tablespoons butter, cut into ½-inch bits, plus 1 teaspoon butter, softened	1 tablespoon sugar
	1½ teaspoons crumbled dried chervil
½ pound small white onions, each about ½ inch in diameter, peeled	1 teaspoon salt
	1 cup water
	1 teaspoon flour

Wash the head of lettuce briefly under cold running water, remove the tough or blemished outer leaves, and cut the lettuce lengthwise into quarters. To shred the lettuce, cut out the core and slice each of the quarters crosswise into ⅛-inch-wide strips.

In a heavy 12-inch skillet, melt the 4 tablespoons of butter bits over moderate heat. When the foam begins to subside, add the onions and turn them with a spoon until they are coated with butter. Drop in the lettuce and toss the shreds about to moisten them evenly. Then add the green peas, sugar, chervil, salt and water and, stirring constantly, bring to a boil over high heat. Reduce the heat to low, cover the skillet tightly and simmer until the peas and onions are tender but still intact. This may take anywhere from 8 to 15 minutes, depending on the size and age of the green peas and the onions.

Blend the teaspoon of softened butter and the flour together in a bowl, add them to the simmering vegetables and stir over moderate heat until the liquid comes to a boil and thickens slightly.

Taste for seasoning and serve the green peas à la française at once from a heated bowl.

Ham-stuffed Eggplant

To serve 4

2 medium-sized eggplants (each about 1 pound)
⅓ cup olive oil
8 tablespoons butter, cut into ½-inch bits, plus 4 teaspoons butter, melted
½ cup finely chopped onions
½ cup finely chopped scallions, including 3 inches of the green tops
1½ teaspoons finely chopped garlic
1 cup coarsely chopped drained canned tomatoes

1 teaspoon crumbled dried thyme
½ teaspoon ground hot red pepper (cayenne)
¼ teaspoon freshly ground black pepper
½ teaspoon salt
½ pound lean smoked ham, finely ground
2¼ cups soft fresh crumbs made from French- or Italian-type white bread, trimmed of all crusts and pulverized in a blender
¼ cup finely chopped fresh parsley, preferably the flat-leaf Italian variety

Cut the eggplants in half lengthwise and, with a spoon, hollow out the center of each half to make a boatlike shell about ¼ inch thick. Finely chop the eggplant pulp and set it aside.

In a heavy 12-inch skillet, heat the olive oil over moderate heat until a light haze forms above it. Add the eggplant shells and turn them about with tongs or a spoon until they are moistened on all sides. Then cover the skillet tightly and cook over moderate heat for 5 or 6 minutes. Turn the shells over and continue to cook, still tightly covered, for 5 minutes longer, or until they are somewhat soft to the touch. Invert the shells on paper towels to drain briefly and arrange them cut side up in a baking dish large enough to hold them snugly in one layer.

Preheat the oven to 400°. Drain off the oil remaining in the skillet, add the 8 tablespoons of butter bits and melt them over moderate heat. When the foam subsides, add the onions, scallions and garlic and, stirring frequently, cook for 5 minutes, or until they are soft but not brown.

Add the reserved chopped eggplant pulp, the tomatoes, thyme, red and black pepper, and salt and, stirring frequently, cook briskly until most of the liquid in the pan evaporates and the mixture is thick enough to hold its shape almost solidly in a spoon. Remove the skillet from the heat and stir in the ground ham, 2 cups of the bread crumbs and the parsley. Taste for seasoning.

Spoon the filling into the eggplant shells, dividing it equally among them and mounding it slightly in the centers. Sprinkle each shell with 1 tablespoon of the remaining bread crumbs and dribble 1 teaspoon of the melted butter on top. Bake in the middle of the oven for 15 minutes, or until the shells are tender and the filling lightly browned. Arrange the ham-stuffed eggplant attractively on a large heated platter or individual plates and serve at once.

Eggplant Soufflé

To serve 4

3 medium-sized eggplants, about
    1 pound each, peeled and cut into
    1½-inch chunks
1 tablespoon butter, softened, plus
    3 tablespoons butter
3 tablespoons plus ½ cup freshly
    grated imported Parmesan cheese
¼ cup finely chopped onions

3 tablespoons flour
1 cup milk
4 egg yolks, lightly beaten
2 tablespoons canned tomato paste
¼ teaspoon ground hot red pepper
    (cayenne)
1 teaspoon salt
6 egg whites

Pour water into the lower part of a steamer to within about 1 inch of the top pan. Bring the water to a boil, put the eggplant chunks in the top pan and set the pan in place. Immediately cover the pan and steam over high heat for 20 to 25 minutes, or until the eggplant is tender.

(If you do not have a steamer, you can improvise one. Use a large pot equipped with a tightly fitting cover, and either a standing colander or a collapsible steaming basket on legs. Pour water into the pot to within about 1 inch of the perforated container and bring it to a boil. Drop the eggplant in the basket or colander, set it in place and cover the pot. Steam over high heat for 20 to 25 minutes, or until the eggplant is tender.)

Purée the eggplant through a food mill or mash it smooth with a fork. Then transfer the purée to a fine sieve and press it firmly with the back of a spoon to extract all its liquid. Set the purée aside. (There should be about 1½ cups of purée.)

Preheat the oven to 400°. With a pastry brush, spread the tablesoon of softened butter over the bottom and sides of a 2-quart soufflé dish. Sprinkle in 3 tablespoons of the grated cheese and tip the dish from side to side to distribute it evenly. Set the soufflé dish aside.

In a heavy 1½- to 2-quart saucepan, melt the remaining 3 tablespoons of butter over moderate heat. When the foam subsides, add the onions and, stirring frequently, cook for about 5 minutes, or until they are soft and translucent but not brown. Add the flour and mix well.

Stirring constantly with a wire whisk, pour in the milk in a slow, thin stream and cook over high heat until the sauce comes to a boil, thickens heavily and is smooth. Reduce the heat to low and simmer for 2 or 3 minutes to remove the raw taste of the flour.

Pour 2 tablespoons of the simmering sauce into the beaten egg yolks, mix well, then stir the yolks into the saucepan and cook over low heat for a minute or so. Do not let the sauce come near a boil or the yolks will curdle. Add the reserved eggplant purée, the remaining ½ cup of cheese, the tomato paste, red pepper and salt. Remove the pan from the heat.

Continued on next page

With a wire whisk or a rotary or electric beater, beat the egg whites until they are stiff enough to stand in unwavering peaks on the whisk or beater when it is lifted from the bowl. With a rubber spatula, scoop the egg whites over the eggplant-and-cheese sauce and fold them together gently but thoroughly.

Pour the mixture into the reserved soufflé dish, spreading it evenly and smoothing the top with the spatula. Place the dish on the middle shelf of the oven and immediately reduce the oven temperature to 375°. Bake for 25 to 30 minutes, or until the soufflé puffs up about 2 inches above the rim of the dish and the top is lightly browned. Serve at once.

Tomato Relish

To make about 4 pints

15 large firm ripe tomatoes (about 7½ pounds)	coarsely chopped
2 medium-sized onions, peeled and coarsely chopped	3 tablespoons sugar
	1 tablespoon salt
1 large red bell pepper, quartered, stemmed, seeded, deribbed and coarsely chopped	3 tablespoons cider vinegar
	1½ teaspoons ground cinnamon
	½ teaspoon ground allspice
1 large green bell pepper, quartered, stemmed, seeded, deribbed and	½ teaspoon ground nutmeg, preferably freshly grated
	½ teaspoon ground cloves

Drop the tomatoes, three or four at a time, into a pan of boiling water and remove them after 15 seconds. Run cold water over them, then cut out the stems and peel the tomatoes with a small sharp knife. Chop the tomatoes coarsely.

Put the tomatoes, onions and red and green peppers through the medium blade of a food grinder and transfer the mixture to a heavy 6- to 8-quart enameled casserole. Stir in the sugar and salt, and bring to a boil over high heat. Stirring frequently, cook briskly, uncovered, until the mixture is reduced to about half its original volume and is thick enough to hold its shape almost solidly in a spoon.

Add the vinegar, cinnamon, allspice, nutmeg and cloves, reduce the heat to low, and partially cover the casserole. Simmer the tomato relish for 1 hour. Immediately ladle the relish into hot sterilized jars, filling them to within ⅛ inch of the tops. Seal the jars at once, following the directions for canning and sealing on page 4.

Mirliton Pickles

To make about 4 pints

5 medium-sized firm ripe mirliton
  squash (about 2½ pounds)
½ pound fresh hot red chilies,
  each about 2 inches long

(caution: see note, page 6)
4 large garlic cloves, peeled
2½ cups cider vinegar
4 teaspoons salt

With a small sharp knife, peel the squash and cut them in half lengthwise. Use the tip of the knife to pry out the seeds from the centers of the squash; discard the seeds. Then cut each squash half lengthwise into slices about ½ inch thick.

Wash the chilies under cold running water and pull out the stems. Slice the chilies lengthwise in half, and then into long ¼-inch-wide strips. Brush away any remaining seeds.

To assemble the pickles, place a clove of garlic in the bottom of each of four hot sterilized pint jars. Arrange the squash and chili alternately in the jars, dividing the slices evenly among them.

Bring the vinegar and salt to a boil in a small enameled or stainless-steel saucepan and immediately ladle the liquid into the jars, a little at a time, allowing it to flow through to the bottom before adding more. Fill the jars to within ⅛ inch of the tops and, following the directions for canning and sealing on page 4, process the jars for 10 minutes in a hot-water bath. Set the mirliton pickles aside in a cool place (preferably not the refrigerator) for at least 10 days before serving.

Dill-Okra Pickles

To make about 2 quarts

1 pound fresh young okra
1 cup cider vinegar
1 cup water
2 tablespoons mustard seeds
2 tablespoons dill seeds

2 tablespoons celery seeds
2 tablespoons crushed dried hot red
  pepper
3 tablespoons salt
16 medium-sized garlic cloves,
  peeled

Wash the okra under cold running water, and with a small sharp knife scrape the skin lightly to remove any surface fuzz. Cut ⅛ inch off the stem at the wide end of each pod. Drop the okra into a large bowl half filled with ice cubes and water and refrigerate for about 1 hour.

Combine the vinegar, 1 cup of water, mustard seeds, dill seeds, celery seeds, red pepper and salt in a 2- to 3-quart enameled or stainless-steel

Continued on next page 111

saucepan. Stirring constantly, bring to a boil over high heat. Remove the pan from the heat and cover to keep the mixture hot.

To assemble the pickles, pat the okra pods completely dry with paper towels and pack the okra and garlic into two hot sterilized quart jars. Ladle in the hot vinegar mixture, a little at a time, allowing the spices to flow through to the bottom of the jars before adding more and filling the jars to within ⅛ inch of the tops.

Following the directions for canning and sealing on page 4, process the jars for 10 minutes in a hot-water bath. Set the dill-okra pickles aside in a cool place (preferably not the refrigerator) for at least 3 weeks before serving.

Jerusalem-Artichoke Pickles

To make about 3 pints

2 tablespoons strained fresh lemon juice	1 teaspoon turmeric
	1 teaspoon dry mustard
2 pounds Jerusalem artichokes	2 teaspoons salt
1 quart cider vinegar	½ small red or green bell pepper,
2 cups sugar	stemmed, seeded, deribbed and
1 teaspoon celery seeds	cut into ½-inch squares

Combine the lemon juice and about 2 quarts of cold water in a deep pot. With a small sharp knife, peel the Jerusalem artichokes and cut them into ½-inch cubes, dropping the cubes into the lemon-water mixture to prevent discoloring as you proceed.

Combine the vinegar, sugar, celery seeds, turmeric, mustard and salt in a 2- to 3-quart enameled or stainless-steel saucepan and bring to a boil over high heat, stirring until the sugar dissolves. Reduce the heat to low and simmer the syrup uncovered for 2 or 3 minutes. Then remove the pan from the heat and stir in the squares of bell pepper.

To assemble the pickles, pack the Jerusalem artichokes tightly into the jars. Ladle in the hot syrup, a little at a time, allowing it to flow through to the bottom of the jars before adding more. Fill the jars to within ⅛ inch of the top and, following the directions for canning and sealing on page 4, process the jars for 10 minutes in a hot-water bath. Set the pickles aside in a cool place (preferably not the refrigerator) for 1 week before serving.

Pickled Peaches

To make 1 quart

2 cups sugar	8 whole allspice
1½ cups cider vinegar	2 two-inch cinnamon sticks
1½ cups water	8 small firm ripe peaches (about
10 whole cloves	2 pounds)

Combine the sugar, vinegar, water, cloves, allspice and cinnamon sticks in a 2- to 3-quart enameled or stainless-steel saucepan and bring to a boil over high heat, stirring until the sugar dissolves. Reduce the heat to low and simmer the syrup, partially covered, for about 10 minutes.

Meanwhile, drop the peaches, three or four at a time, into enough boiling water to cover them completely. Boil briskly for 2 or 3 minutes, then transfer the peaches to a sieve or colander. Drain and peel them with a small sharp knife.

Place the peaches in a hot sterilized quart jar and ladle the hot syrup over them, a little at a time, letting the spices flow through to the bottom of the jar before adding more. Fill the jar to within ⅛ inch of the top and discard any excess syrup. Following the directions for canning and sealing on page 4, process the jars for 10 minutes in a hot-water bath. Set the pickled peaches aside in a cool place for a least 1 week before serving.

Blackberry Jam

To make about 5 cups

	½ cup water
6 cups fresh ripe blackberries	4 cups sugar

Pick over the berries carefully, removing any stems and discarding fruit that is badly bruised or shows signs of mold. Do not discard any under-ripe berries; although tarter than ripe ones, they contain more pectin —the substance that jells the fruit.

Wash the blackberries briefly in a large sieve or colander set under cold running water and drop them into a heavy 4- to 6-quart enameled casserole. Add the water and sugar, and bring to a boil over high heat, stirring until the sugar dissolves. Reduce the heat to moderate and, stirring from time to time, cook uncovered until the jam reaches a temperature of 221° (or 9° above the boiling point of water in your locality) on a jelly, candy or deep-frying thermometer.

Remove the pan from the heat. With a large spoon, carefully skim off the foam from the surface and ladle the blackberry jam into hot sterilized jars. For canning and sealing directions see the Recipe Index.

Pain Perdu

To serve 4

5 eggs	peel
½ cup granulated sugar	8 half-inch-thick slices of day-old
3 tablespoons brandy	French- or Italian-type bread
2 tablespoons orange-flower water	1 pound lard
1 teaspoon finely grated fresh lemon	Confectioners' sugar

The name pain perdu, which literally means "lost bread," refers to the fact that the dish is made with stale bread that might otherwise be discarded. Even in this rather elaborate version of the recipe, it is clear that pain perdu is related to our familiar French toast.

In a large, deep bowl, beat the eggs and granulated sugar with a wire whisk or a rotary or electric beater until they are frothy and well combined. Beat in the brandy, orange-flower water and lemon peel, then add the bread slices and turn them about in the egg mixture to moisten them evenly. Let the bread soak at room temperature for at least 30 minutes.

In a heavy 12-inch skillet, melt the lard over moderate heat until it is very hot but not smoking. Fry the bread, three or four slices at a time, for 2 minutes on each side, turning the slices carefully with a wide metal spatula and regulating the heat so that they brown richly and evenly without burning. As they brown, transfer the bread slices to paper towels to drain.

Sprinkle the *pain perdu* with confectioners' sugar and serve at once, accompanied, if you like, by a pitcher of pure cane syrup *(see Glossary)*.

Beignets
FRENCH-TYPE DOUGHNUT SQUARES

To make 10 five-inch square
  doughnuts

¼ cup lukewarm water (110° to
  115°)
1 package active dry yeast
¼ cup granulated sugar
2 tablespoons vegetable shortening

½ teaspoon salt
½ cup boiling water
½ cup heavy cream
1 egg, lightly beaten
4 to 4½ cups unsifted flour
Vegetable oil for deep frying
Confectioners' sugar

Pour the lukewarm water into a shallow bowl and sprinkle the yeast over it. Let the yeast rest for 2 or 3 minutes, then mix well. Set in a warm, draft-free place (such as an unlighted oven) for about 10 minutes, or until the yeast bubbles up and the mixture almost doubles in bulk.

Meanwhile, combine the granulated sugar, shortening and salt in a deep bowl. Pour in the boiling water and stir with a wooden spoon until the ingredients are thoroughly blended and the mixture has cooled to luke-warm (110° to 115°). Stir in the heavy cream, the yeast mixture and the egg. Add 2 cups of the flour and, when it is completely incorporated, beat in up to 2½ cups more flour, ¼ cup at a time. Add only enough flour to make the dough smooth and not sticky. When the dough be-comes too stiff to stir easily with the spoon, work in the additional flour with your fingers.

Pour vegetable oil into a deep fryer or large heavy saucepan to a depth of 2 to 3 inches and heat the oil until it reaches a temperature of 360° on a deep-frying thermometer.

Gather the dough into a ball, place it on a lightly floured surface and pat it into a rectangle about 1 inch thick. Dust a little flour over and under the dough and roll it out from the center to within an inch of the far edge. Lift the dough and turn it at right angles, then roll again from the center as before. Repeat—lifting, turning, rolling—until the rectangle is about ¼ inch thick and at least 25 inches long by 10 inches wide. If the dough sticks to the board, lift it with a wide metal spatula and sprinkle a little flour under it.

With a pastry wheel or sharp knife, cut the dough into 10 five-inch square *beignets* and deep-fry them immediately. Drop the *beignets,* two or three at a time, into the hot oil and turn them over with a slotted spoon as soon as they rise to the surface. Continue deep-frying, turning the *beignets* frequently, for about 3 to 5 minutes, or until they are crisp and golden brown on all sides. As they brown, transfer the *beignets* to paper towels to drain.

Sprinkle the *beignets* lightly with the confectioners' sugar and serve them at once while they are still hot.

Calas

DEEP-FRIED RICE BALLS

To make 6 balls

	1 teaspoon ground cinnamon
1½ cups water	1 teaspoon ground nutmeg,
⅔ cup uncooked white rice, not	preferably freshly grated
the converted variety	¼ teaspoon salt
1½ cups unsifted flour	2 eggs
1½ teaspoons double-acting	2 tablespoons sugar
baking powder	Vegetable oil for deep frying

Before the turn of the century, the cala woman vending "Belle cala! Tout chaud!" ("Nice cala! Piping hot!") was a familiar sight along the streets of the French Quarter of New Orleans. The cala women have disappeared, but these unique deep-fried rice balls are still available, fresh and hot, at Maxcy's Coffee Pot Restaurant in the heart of the Quarter.

Bring the water to a boil in a small heavy saucepan set over high heat. Pour in the rice in a slow, thin stream, stir two or three times, then cover the pan tightly. Reduce the heat to low and simmer for 15 minutes, or until the rice has absorbed all of the liquid in the pan and the grains are plump and tender. Spread out the rice in a large shallow pan and let it cool to room temperature.

Meanwhile, combine the flour, baking powder, cinnamon, nutmeg and salt, sift them together into a bowl, and set aside.

In a deep bowl, beat the eggs and sugar for 2 or 3 minutes with a wire whisk or a rotary or electric beater. Add the cooled rice and stir briskly with a spoon until the grains are separated and evenly coated with the egg-and-sugar mixture. Add the flour mixture ½ cup at a time, stirring the dough well after each addition.

Divide the rice dough into six equal portions and, moistening your hands frequently with cold water, pat and shape each portion into a ball about 2½ inches in diameter. As you proceed, place the balls side by side on wax paper.

Pour the vegetable oil into a deep fryer or large heavy saucepan to a depth of about 3 inches and heat the oil until it reaches a temperature of 350° on a deep-frying thermometer.

Deep-fry the rice balls, two or three at a time, turning them about with a slotted spoon for about 8 minutes, or until they are golden brown and crusty. As they brown, transfer the rice balls to paper towels to drain while you deep-fry the rest.

Arrange the calas attractively on a heated platter and serve them while they are still hot. Calas are traditionally served at breakfast, accompanied by cane syrup or jelly or sprinkled with a little confectioners' sugar or a mixture of granulated sugar and cinnamon.

Rice Fritters

To make about 1 dozen 2-inch
 fritters

⅔ cup water
⅓ cup uncooked long-grain white
 rice, not the converted variety
½ cup flour
2 tablespoons granulated sugar

1 teaspoon double-acting baking
 powder
⅛ teaspoon salt
Vegetable oil for deep frying
3 eggs

Bring the water to a boil in a small heavy saucepan set over high heat. Pour in the rice in a slow, thin stream, stir two or three times, then cover the pan tightly. Reduce the heat to low and simmer for 15 minutes, or until the rice has absorbed all of the liquid in the pan and the grains are plump and tender.

Meanwhile, combine the flour, granulated sugar, baking powder and salt. Sift them together into a bowl and set aside.

Pour vegetable oil into a deep fryer or large heavy saucepan to a depth of about 3 inches and heat the oil until it reaches a temperature of 350° on a deep-frying thermometer.

When the rice has cooked its allotted time, purée it through a food mill or potato ricer set over a deep bowl. With the back of a fork, mash the rice purée to a smooth, thick paste. Break in the eggs, one at a time, and beat well after each addition. Then gradually incorporate the reserved flour mixture and continue to beat until the batter is smooth.

For each fritter, drop a tablespoon of the batter directly into the hot oil. Allow enough space between them so that they can puff into 2-inch balls. Deep-fry three or four at a time, turning them with a slotted spoon, for about 3 minutes, or until they are golden brown and crisp. As they brown, transfer the fritters to paper towels to drain while you deep-fry the rest.

Arrange the fritters attractively on a heated platter and serve them while they are still hot. At breakfast, the rice fritters are traditionally sprinkled with confectioners' sugar or topped with cane syrup. When served at lunch or dinner, they are eaten plain.

French Bread

To make three 16-inch-long loaves

2¼ cups lukewarm water (110°
　to 115°)
1 package active dry yeast
1 teaspoon sugar
7 to 8 cups unsifted all-purpose
　flour

1 tablespoon salt plus ½ teaspoon
　salt dissolved in ½ cup water
1 tablespoon butter, softened, or
　substitute 1 tablespoon vegetable
　oil
½ cup white or yellow cornmeal

Pour ¼ cup of the lukewarm water into a small bowl and sprinkle in the yeast and sugar. Let the yeast and sugar rest for 2 or 3 minutes, then mix well. Set in a warm, draft-free place (such as an unlighted oven) for about 10 minutes, or until the yeast bubbles up and the mixture almost doubles in volume.

Place 7 cups of the flour and 1 tablespoon of salt in a deep mixing bowl and make a well in the center. Pour the yeast mixture and the remaining 2 cups of lukewarm water into the well and, with a large wooden spoon, gradually incorporate the dry ingredients into the water. Then stir with the spoon until the dough can be gathered into a medium-firm ball.

Place the ball on a lightly floured surface and knead, pushing the dough down with the heels of your hands, pressing it forward and folding it back on itself. As you knead, incorporate up to 1 cup more flour, adding it by the tablespoonful and using only enough to make a non-sticky dough. Continue to knead for 10 to 15 minutes, or until the dough is smooth and elastic.

With a pastry brush, spread the softened butter or vegetable oil over the inside of a large bowl. Set the dough in the bowl and turn it about in the grease to coat the entire surface. Drape the bowl with a kitchen towel and set it aside in the draft-free place for approximately 1½ hours, or until the dough doubles in volume.

Scatter the cornmeal on a large baking sheet and set the sheet aside. Then punch the dough down with a blow of your fist and divide it into three equal portions. On a lightly floured surface, roll and shape each portion into a slightly tapered loaf about 2 inches in diameter and 15 inches long. Place the loaves 2 inches apart on the cornmeal-coated baking sheet. With a very sharp knife make six diagonal slashes, each about 2 inches long and ½ inch deep, at 1½-inch intervals in the center part of the top of each loaf. Brush the three loaves with 2 tablespoons of the salt-and-water solution and set them aside in the warm, draft-free place for about 45 minutes longer, or until they double in volume.

Preheat the oven to 400° and place a large shallow pan half filled with boiling water on the oven floor or, if your oven is electric, directly on the bottom heating unit. Bake the bread on the lowest shelf of the oven for 15 minutes. Then reduce the oven temperature to 350°, brush the loaves with the salt-and-water solution and bake for 10 minutes. Brush again with the salt water and continue to bake the bread for about 20 minutes longer, or until the loaves are crisp and golden. Remove from the baking sheet and let the loaves cool on a wire rack before serving.

Coush-Coush
FRIED CORNMEAL

To serve 4

2 cups yellow cornmeal, preferably the water-ground variety	powder
	2 teaspoons sugar
½ cup unsifted flour	2 teaspoons salt
1 tablespoon double-acting baking	1½ cups water
	8 tablespoons lard

Combine the cornmeal, flour, baking powder, sugar and salt in a deep bowl and stir with a wooden spoon until all the ingredients are thoroughly combined. Pour in the water and stir vigorously to make a smooth, thick paste.

In a heavy 9- to 10-inch cast-iron skillet, melt the lard over moderate heat until it is hot but not smoking. Add the cornmeal mixture and pat it flat in the skillet with the back of the spoon. Then increase the heat to high and fry the cornmeal cake for 10 to 12 minutes, or until it is brown and crusty on the bottom.

Stir the cornmeal mixture to distribute the bits of brown crust evenly through it. Reduce the heat to low, cover the skillet tightly, and cook the coush-coush for 15 minutes longer.

Spoon the coush-coush into heated individual bowls and serve at once, as a breakfast cereal.

Coush-coush is traditionally accompanied by milk and sugar, or by pure cane syrup *(see Glossary)*.

Dessert Crêpes

To make 8 or 9 eight-inch crêpes

½ cup flour
1 tablespoon sugar
⅛ teaspoon salt
2 eggs

½ cup milk
¼ teaspoon vanilla extract
½ teaspoon finely grated fresh
    orange peel (optional)
2 to 4 tablespoons butter, melted

To make the crêpe batter in an electric blender, combine the flour, sugar, salt, eggs, milk and vanilla extract in the blender jar. Blend at high speed for a few seconds. Turn off the machine, scrape down the sides of the jar with a rubber spatula and blend again for about 30 seconds. Pour the batter into a deep bowl and stir in the grated orange peel.

To make the crêpe batter by hand, stir the flour, sugar, salt and eggs together in a mixing bowl and gradually mix in the milk and vanilla extract. Beat with a wire whisk or a rotary or electric beater until the flour lumps disappear, then rub the batter through a fine sieve into another bowl and stir in the grated orange peel.

Cover the bowl tightly with foil or plastic wrap and let the batter rest at room temperature for at least one hour before using it. To fry the crêpes, warm an 8-inch crêpe pan or skillet over high heat until a drop of water flicked into it splutters and evaporates instantly. With a hair-bristle (not nylon) pastry brush, lightly grease the bottom and sides of the heated pan with a little of the melted butter.

Stir the crêpe batter lightly with a wire whisk or a spoon. Then, using a small ladle, pour about ¼ cup of the batter into the pan. Tip the pan from side to side so that the batter quickly covers the bottom; the batter will cling to the pan and begin to firm up almost immediately. At once tilt the pan over the bowl and pour off any excess batter; the finished crêpe should be paper thin.

Cook the crêpe for a minute or so until a rim of brown shows around the edge. Turn it over with a spatula and cook the other side for a minute longer. Slide the crêpe onto a plate. Brush melted butter on the pan again and make the remaining crêpes similarly.

As the crêpes are finished, stack them one upon the other. The crêpes may be made ahead of time and kept, covered with plastic wrap, at room temperature. If you like, you may freeze the crêpes; but in this event return them to room temperature before separating them.

Crêpes Fitzgerald

To serve 4

6 ounces (¾ cup) cream cheese,
  cut into small bits and softened
¾ cup sour cream
4 tablespoons sugar
1 tablespoon finely grated fresh
  lemon peel
8 dessert crêpes *(opposite)*,
  thoroughly defrosted if frozen

2 cups frozen unsweetened whole
  strawberries, thoroughly
  defrosted and drained
  (26 ounces)
8 tablespoons unsalted butter
  (1 quarter-pound stick), cut into
  ½-inch bits
¼ cup strawberry liqueur
¼ cup kirsch liqueur

These unusual stuffed crêpes, created at Brennan's Restaurant in 1958, are still a feature of their menu. The dessert was named in honor of six members of the staff of Fitzgerald Advertising, Inc., who lunched together at the restaurant every day.

In a deep bowl, cream the cream cheese by beating and mashing it against the sides of the bowl with the back of a large spoon until the cheese is light and fluffy. Beat in the sour cream and, when it is well incorporated, add 2 tablespoons of the sugar and the grated lemon peel.

Spoon 2 tablespoons of the cream-cheese mixture on the lower third of each crêpe and roll the crêpes up into tight cylinders; do not tuck in the ends. Set the filled crêpes aside.

With the back of a fork or spoon, mash the strawberries to a smooth purée. Melt 4 tablespoons of the butter bits in a small heavy saucepan set over moderate heat. When the foam begins to subside, add the puréed strawberries, the strawberry liqueur and the remaining 2 tablespoons of sugar. Bring to a boil, stirring until the sugar dissolves completely, then cover the pan tightly and set the strawberry sauce aside off the heat.

In a heavy 12-inch skillet, melt the remaining 4 tablespoons of butter bits over moderate heat. Add the crêpes and, turning them gently with a spoon, cook for 2 or 3 minutes to heat them through.

Pour the kirsch liqueur over the crêpes carefully. It may ignite spontaneously; if not, let it warm for a moment or two, then ignite it with a match. Slide the pan back and forth over the heat until the flames die.

Immediately transfer the crêpes to a heated serving platter and pour the strawberry sauce over them. Serve at once.

Jelly Crêpes

To serve 4

1 cup blackberry or apple jelly
8 dessert crêpes (*page 120*),
   thoroughly defrosted if frozen
8 tablespoons unsalted butter
   (1 quarter-pound stick), cut into
   ½-inch bits

The peel of 2 oranges, cut into
   strips about 1 inch long and
   ¼ inch wide
½ cup curaçao or other orange-
   flavored liqueur
½ cup cognac
1 cup slivered blanched almonds

Spoon 2 tablespoons of the jelly on the lower third of each crêpe and roll the crêpes up into tight cylinders; do not tuck in the ends.

In a heavy 12-inch skillet, melt the butter bits over moderate heat. When the foam begins to subside, stir in the orange peel. Then add the crêpes and, turning them gently with a spoon, cook for 2 or 3 minutes to heat them through.

Pour the liqueur and cognac over the crêpes carefully; they may ignite spontaneously. If not, let the liqueur and cognac warm for a few moments, then ignite them with a match. Slide the pan back and forth over the heat until the flames die.

With a slotted spatula, transfer the crêpes to a heated serving platter. Drop the almonds into the sauce remaining in the skillet and stir for a minute or two. As soon as the almonds are hot and evenly coated with sauce, pour them over the crêpes. Serve at once.

Bananas Foster

To serve 4

1 pint vanilla ice cream
8 tablespoons butter, cut into
   ½-inch bits
½ cup brown sugar

4 firm ripe bananas, peeled and cut
   lengthwise into halves
½ teaspoon ground cinnamon
½ cup banana liqueur
1 cup rum

This elegant dessert of flamed bananas and ice cream, created at Brennan's over 20 years ago for a regular patron named Richard Foster, has become one of the restaurant's most popular dishes.

Prepare and assemble the bananas Foster at the dinner table when you are ready to serve them. Light an alcohol burner or table-top stove and set a 12-inch copper *flambé* or crêpe-suzette pan over the flame. Arrange all the ingredients conveniently beside the pan. Place a scoop of ice cream on each of four chilled individual dessert plates and set them to one side.

Combine the butter and brown sugar in the *flambé* pan and stir until the mixture becomes a smooth syrup. Add the bananas and baste them with the syrup for 3 or 4 minutes, then sprinkle in the cinnamon.

Carefully pour in the banana liqueur and rum, and let the liquors warm for a few seconds. They may burst into flame spontaneously. If not, ignite them with a match. Slide the pan back and forth until the flames die, basting the bananas all the while. Place two banana halves around each scoop of ice cream, spoon the sauce over the top and serve at once.

Cherries Jubilee

To serve 4

A 1-pound can pitted sweet Bing cherries, drained, with all their liquid reserved	1 tablespoon cold water
1 tablespoon cornstarch mixed with	¼ cup kirsch liqueur
	¼ cup maraschino liqueur
	1 pint vanilla ice cream

Pour the cherry liquid into a small saucepan and bring it to a simmer over moderate heat. Stirring constantly, add the cornstarch-and-water mixture and cook until the sauce comes to a boil, thickens lightly and is smooth. Remove the pan from the heat and let the sauce cool to room temperature, then cover tightly and set it aside.

Prepare and assemble the cherries jubilee at the dinner table, when you are ready to serve them. Light an alcohol burner or table-top stove and set a 12-inch copper *flambé* or crêpe suzette pan over the flame. Arrange the cherry sauce, cherries, kirsch and maraschino conveniently beside the pan. Place a scoop of ice cream in each of four chilled individual dessert bowls and set them to one side.

Drop the cherries into the *flambé* pan and stir until they are heated. Carefully pour the kirsch and maraschino into the pan, step back from the table and let the liqueurs warm for a few seconds. They may burst into flame spontaneously. If not, ignite them with a match.

Gently slide the pan back and forth over the heat until the flames die, basting the cherries all the while with the liqueurs. Then stir in the cherry sauce and cook briefly to heat it through.

Ladle the cherries and sauce over the ice cream and serve at once.

Bread Pudding with Whiskey Sauce

To serve 8 to 10

PUDDING

2 tablespoons butter, softened	3 eggs
A 12-ounce loaf day-old French- or Italian-type white bread	2 cups sugar
	½ cup seedless raisins
1 quart milk	2 tablespoons vanilla extract

Preheat the oven to 350°. With a pastry brush, spread the softened butter evenly over the bottom and sides of a 13-by-9-by-2-inch baking-serving dish. Set the dish aside.

Break the bread into chunks, dropping them into a bowl as you proceed, and pour milk over them. When the bread is softened, crumble it into small bits and let it continue to soak until all the milk is absorbed.

In a small bowl, beat 3 eggs and 2 cups of sugar together with a wire whisk or a rotary or electric beater until the mixture is smooth and thick. Stir in the raisins and vanilla extract, then pour the egg mixture over the bread crumbs and stir until all the ingredients are well combined.

Pour the bread pudding into the buttered dish, spreading it evenly and smoothing the top with a rubber spatula. Place the dish in a large shallow roasting pan set on the middle shelf of the oven and pour boiling water into the pan to a depth of about 1 inch. Bake for 1 hour, or until a knife inserted in the center of the pudding comes out clean.

SAUCE

8 tablespoons butter (1 quarter-pound stick), cut into ½-inch bits	1 cup sugar
	1 egg
	½ cup bourbon

Meanwhile, prepare the sauce in the following fashion: Melt the butter bits in the top of a double boiler set over hot, not boiling, water. Stir 1 cup of sugar and 1 egg together in a small bowl and add the mixture to the butter. Stir for 2 or 3 minutes, until the sugar dissolves completely and the egg is cooked, but do not let the sauce come anywhere near a boil or the egg will curdle. Remove the pan from the heat and let the sauce cool to room temperature before stirring in the bourbon.

Serve the bread pudding at once, directly from the baking dish, and present the whiskey sauce separately in a sauceboat or small bowl.

Tourtes Douces

BLACKBERRY TURNOVERS

To make 2 dozen 8-inch turnovers

5 cups unsifted flour
2 teaspoons double-acting baking powder
1 teaspoon salt
1 teaspoon vanilla extract
¾ cup milk

10 tablespoons butter, softened
8 tablespoons vegetable shortening, softened
1½ cups granulated sugar
2 eggs
5 cups blackberry jam *(page 113)*
Confectioners' sugar

Combine the flour, baking powder and salt and sift them into a bowl. Add the vanilla extract to the milk and set the mixture aside.

In a deep bowl, cream 8 tablespoons of the softened butter, the vegetable shortening and granulated sugar together by beating and mashing them against the sides of the bowl with the back of a large spoon until the mixture is light and fluffy. Beat in the eggs, one at a time. Add about 1½ cups of the flour mixture and, when it is well incorporated, beat in about ¼ cup of the milk mixture. Repeat two more times, alternating about 1½ cups of the flour with ¼ cup of the milk and beating well after each addition.

Divide the dough into 24 equal portions and pat and shape each portion into a ball. Arrange the balls in one layer in a shallow dish, drape wax paper over them, and refrigerate for about 1 hour for easier rolling.

Meanwhile, warm the blackberry jam in a small saucepan, stirring frequently until it is fluid. Pour the jam through a fine sieve set over a bowl to strain out the seeds, then let the jam cool to room temperature.

Preheat the oven to 375°. With a pastry brush, spread the remaining 2 tablespoons of softened butter evenly over two large baking sheets. To shape each turnover, place one ball of dough at a time on a lightly floured surface and roll it into a circle about 8 inches in diameter. Spoon about 3 tablespoons of the blackberry jam onto the center of each circle and spread it evenly, leaving at least ½ inch of dough exposed around it.

Moisten the exposed dough with a finger dipped in water and fold the circle over to make a half-moon shape. With the tines of a fork, crimp the curved edges tightly together and pierce the top of the turnover in two or three places. As you proceed, arrange the turnovers side by side on the buttered baking sheets.

Bake in the middle of the oven for 20 minutes, or until the *tourtes douces* are delicately browned. With a spatula, transfer them to wire racks to cool to room temperature. Just before serving, sprinkle the turnovers lightly with confectioners' sugar.

Gâteau de Sirop
SYRUP CAKE

To make one 9-inch square cake

9 tablespoons butter, softened
2 tablespoons plus 2½ cups
  unsifted flour
1½ teaspoons double-acting
  baking powder
½ teaspoon baking soda
1 teaspoon ground ginger
1 teaspoon ground cinnamon
¼ teaspoon ground nutmeg,
  preferably freshly grated

¼ teaspoon ground cloves
½ teaspoon salt
½ cup coarsely chopped pecans
½ cup seedless raisins
1 cup pure cane syrup *(see Glossary,*
  page 150), or substitute ⅔ cup
  dark corn syrup mixed with ⅓
  cup dark molasses
1 cup boiling water
½ cup sugar
2 eggs

Preheat the oven to 350°. With a pastry brush, spread 1 tablespoon of the softened butter over the bottom and sides of a 9-by-9-by-2-inch baking pan. Add 1 tablespoon of the flour and tip the pan from side to side to distribute it evenly. Invert the pan and rap the bottom sharply to remove the excess flour.

Combine 2½ cups of the flour, the baking powder, baking soda, ginger, cinnamon, nutmeg, cloves and salt, and sift them together into a mixing bowl. In a separate bowl, mix the remaining tablespoon of flour with the chopped pecans and raisins. Pour the syrup and boiling water into another bowl and mix the liquids well.

In a deep bowl, cream the remaining 8 tablespoons of softened butter and the sugar together by beating and mashing them against the sides of the bowl with the back of a large spoon until the mixture is light and fluffy. Beat in the eggs, one at a time.

Add about ⅔ cup of flour-and-spice mixture and, when it is well incorporated, beat in ½ cup of the syrup mixture. Repeat three more times, alternating about ⅔ cup of the flour-and-spice mixture with ½ cup of the syrup mixture, and beating well after each addition. Add the floured pecans and the raisins and, with a rubber spatula, fold them in gently but thoroughly.

Pour the batter into the prepared pan, spreading it evenly and smoothing the top with the spatula. Bake the syrup cake in the middle of the oven for 50 to 60 minutes, or until a toothpick or cake tester inserted in the center comes out clean.

Cool and serve the syrup cake from the pan or, if you prefer, turn it out on a wire rack to cool and serve the cake from a plate.

Fig Cake

To make one 10-inch tube cake

9 tablespoons butter, softened
2 tablespoons plus 2½ cups
    unsifted flour
1 teaspoon baking soda
1 teaspoon double-acting baking
    powder
1 teaspoon ground cinnamon
1 teaspoon ground nutmeg,
    preferably freshly grated

½ teaspoon salt
4 one-pound cans figs, drained,
    patted dry with paper towels and
    finely chopped
1 cup sugar
3 eggs
1 cup milk
1 tablespoon cider vinegar
1 teaspoon vanilla extract

Preheat the oven to 350°. With a pastry brush, spread 1 tablespoon of the softened butter over the bottom and sides of a 10-inch tube cake pan. Add 2 tablespoons of the flour and tip the pan from side to side to distribute the flour evenly. Then invert the pan and rap the bottom sharply to remove the excess flour.

Sift the remaining 2½ cups of flour and the baking soda, baking powder, cinnamon, nutmeg and salt together into a bowl. Place the figs in another bowl, stir in about ½ cup of the flour mixture, and set aside.

In a deep bowl, cream the remaining 8 tablespoons of softened butter and the sugar together by beating and mashing them against the sides of the bowl with the back of a spoon until the mixture is light and fluffy. Beat in the eggs, one at a time. Add ½ cup of the remaining flour mixture and, when it is well incorporated, beat in ¼ cup of the milk. Repeat three more times, alternating ½ cup of the flour mixture with ¼ cup of the milk and beating well after each addition. Stir in the vinegar and vanilla extract. Then, with a rubber spatula, gently fold the reserved floured figs into the batter.

Pour the batter into the prepared tube pan, spreading it evenly and smoothing the top with the spatula. Bake in the middle of the oven for about 1 hour, or until a toothpick or cake tester inserted into the center of the cake comes out clean.

Let the fig cake cool in the pan for about 10 minutes before turning it out on a wire rack to cool completely to room temperature. Wrap the cake tightly in foil and let it rest at room temperature for at least 24 hours before serving.

Kings' Cake

To make one 12-inch ring

CAKE

½ cup lukewarm water (110° to 115°)

2 packages active dry yeast

2 teaspoons plus ½ cup granulated sugar

3½ to 4½ cups unsifted flour

1 teaspoon ground nutmeg, preferably freshly grated

2 teaspoons salt

1 teaspoon finely grated fresh lemon peel

½ cup lukewarm milk (110° to 115°)

5 egg yolks

8 tablespoons butter (1 quarter-pound stick), cut into ½-inch bits and softened, plus 2 tablespoons butter, softened

½ cup finely chopped candied citron

1 shelled pecan half or uncooked dried bean

1 egg, lightly beaten with 1 tablespoon milk

The New Orleans carnival season begins on January 6, or Twelfth Night, and ends with the revel of Mardi Gras, on the day before Lent begins. Kings' cake is baked for Twelfth Night celebrations—and the lucky person who finds the pecan or bean in his slice of cake is "king or queen for a day." Traditionally, the cake is decorated with sugar tinted in the classic carnival colors: green, purple and yellow.

To make the cake, pour the lukewarm water into a small shallow bowl and sprinkle the yeast and 2 teaspoons of the granulated sugar over it. Let the yeast and sugar rest for 2 to 3 minutes, then stir to mix the ingredients well. Set in a warm, draft-free place (such as an unlighted oven) for about 10 minutes, or until the yeast bubbles up and the mixture almost doubles in volume.

Combine 3½ cups of flour, the remaining ½ cup of granulated sugar, the nutmeg and the salt, and sift them into a deep mixing bowl. Stir in the lemon peel, then make a well in the center and into it pour the yeast mixture and the milk.

Add the egg yolks and, with a large wooden spoon, gradually incorporate the dry ingredients into the liquid ones. When the mixture is smooth, beat in the 8 tablespoons of butter bits, a tablespoonful at a time. Continue to beat for about 2 minutes longer, or until the dough can be gathered into a medium-soft ball.

Place the ball on a lightly floured surface and knead, pushing the dough down with the heels of your hands, pressing it forward and folding it back on itself. As you knead, incorporate up to 1 cup more flour, sprinkling it over the ball by the tablespoonful. When the dough is no longer sticky, knead it for about 10 minutes longer, or until it is smooth, shiny and elastic.

With a pastry brush, spread 1 tablespoon of softened butter evenly over the inside of a large bowl. Set the dough in the bowl and turn it about to butter the entire surface. Drape the bowl with a kitchen towel and put it in the draft-free place for 1½ hours, or until the dough doubles in volume.

Brush a large baking sheet with the remaining tablespoon of softened butter. Punch the dough down with a blow of your fist and place it on a lightly floured surface. Scatter the citron over the top, knead the dough until the citron is well distributed, then pat and shape it into a cylinder about 14 inches long. Loop the cylinder onto the buttered baking sheet and pinch the ends together to form a ring.

Press the pecan half or dried bean gently into the ring so that it is completely hidden by the dough. Drape the dough with the towel again and set it in the draft-free place to rise for about 45 minutes, or until the ring doubles in volume.

Preheat the oven to 375°. (If you have used the oven to let the dough rise, transfer the ring to another warm place to rest while the oven heats.) Brush the top and sides of the ring with the egg-and-milk mixture and bake the Kings' cake in the middle of the oven for 25 to 30 minutes, or until it is golden brown.

Slide the cake onto a wire rack to cool to room temperature.

SUGARS
Green, purple and yellow food-
    coloring pastes
12 tablespoons granulated sugar

Meanwhile, prepare the colored sugars. Squeeze a dot of green coloring paste onto the center of the palm of one hand. Sprinkle 2 tablespoons of granulated sugar over the paste and rub your palms together briskly until the sugar is evenly green. Add more paste if the color is too light and rub the sugar a few minutes longer. Place the green sugar on a saucer or piece of wax paper and repeat the entire procedure again to color 2 more tablespoons of the sugar.

Wash your hands, squeeze a blob of purple food coloring paste on one palm and in a similar fashion color 4 tablespoons of the granulated sugar purple. Wash your hands again and, using the yellow food coloring paste, tint the remaining 4 tablespoons of granulated sugar yellow. Set the green, purple and yellow sugars aside.

Continued on next page

ICING

3 cups confectioners' sugar
¼ cup strained fresh lemon juice   2 candied cherries, cut lengthwise
3 to 6 tablespoons water   into halves

When the cake has cooled, prepare the icing. Combine the confectioners' sugar, lemon juice and 3 tablespoons of the water in a deep bowl and stir until the icing mixture is smooth. If the icing is too stiff to spread easily, beat in up to 3 tablespoons more water, 1 teaspoonful at a time. With a small metal spatula, spread the icing over the top of the cake, allowing it to run irregularly down the sides.

Sprinkle the colored sugars over the icing immediately, forming a row of purple, yellow and green strips, each about 2 inches wide, on both sides of the ring as shown in the photograph on page 44. Arrange two cherry halves at each end of the cake, pressing them gently into the icing.

NOTE: Food coloring pastes are available at bakers' supply stores or by mail (*see Shopping Guide, page 150*). Do not use liquid food coloring, which makes the sugar dissolve and clump and does not color the granules evenly.

Strawberry Ice Cream

To make about 2 quarts

     1 cup sugar
2 quarts firm ripe fresh strawberries   ⅛ teaspoon salt
1 quart heavy cream   1 tablespoon vanilla extract

Pick over the berries carefully, removing the stems and hulls and discarding any fruit that is badly bruised or shows signs of mold. Wash the fruit briefly in a large sieve or colander set under cold running water, then spread the strawberries on paper towels to drain and pat them completely dry with fresh paper towels. Quarter the berries, dropping them into a deep bowl as you proceed.

In a heavy 2- to 3-quart saucepan, heat 1 cup of the cream, the sugar and the salt over low heat, stirring until the sugar is dissolved; do not let the mixture come to a boil. Pour the mixture into a deep bowl, stir in the remaining 3 cups of cream, the vanilla extract and 2 cups of the quartered berries, and refrigerate until the mixture is chilled. Cover the remaining strawberries tightly with foil or plastic wrap and refrigerate until you are ready to use them.

Pack a 2-quart ice-cream freezer with layers of finely crushed or cracked ice and coarse rock salt in the proportions recommended by the freezer manufacturer. Add cold water if the manufacturer advises it. Then ladle the chilled cream mixture into the ice-cream can and cover it.

If you have a hand ice-cream maker, fill it with the chilled cream mixture and let it stand for 3 or 4 minutes before beginning to turn the handle. Then, slowly at first, crank continuously for about 5 minutes. Stir in the reserved strawberries and the liquid that has accumulated around them and crank for 10 to 15 minutes more. Do not stop turning at any time or the ice cream may be lumpy.

When the handle can barely be moved, the ice cream is ready to serve. If you wish to keep it for an hour or two, remove the lid and dasher. Scrape the ice cream off the dasher and pack it firmly into the container with a spoon. Cover securely, pour off any water in the bucket and repack the ice and salt solidly around it.

If you have an electric ice-cream maker, fill the can with the chilled cream mixture, cover it, turn on the switch and let the mixture churn for about 5 minutes. Stir in the reserved strawberries and their liquid, cover again and continue to churn for about 10 to 15 minutes more, or until the motor slows or actually stops. Serve the ice cream immediately or follow the procedure above to keep it for an hour or two.

Lacking an ice-cream maker, stir the reserved berries and liquid into the chilled cream mixture and pour the mixture into four ice-cube trays from which the dividers have been removed. Spread the ice cream evenly and smooth the top with a rubber spatula. Freeze for 3 to 4 hours, stirring every 30 minutes or so and scraping into the ice cream the ice particles that form around the edges of the tray.

Tightly covered, the strawberry ice cream may safely be kept in the freezer or the freezing compartment of the refrigerator for several weeks. Before serving it, place the ice cream in the refrigerator for 20 to 30 minutes to let it soften slightly.

Fig Ice Cream

To make 3 quarts

4 one-pound cans figs, drained	1 cup sugar
2 cups milk	1 teaspoon vanilla extract
⅛ teaspoon salt	4 egg whites
6 egg yolks	2 cups heavy cream

Place the figs in a deep bowl and, with the back of a fork or a large spoon, mash them to a somewhat coarse purée. Cover the bowl with foil or plastic wrap and set the figs aside.

In a heavy 2- to 3-quart saucepan, warm the milk and salt over low heat until bubbles begin to appear around the sides of the pan. Remove the pan from the heat and cover it to keep the milk warm.

With a wire whisk or a rotary or electric beater, beat the egg yolks and sugar together for 4 to 5 minutes, or until they are thick enough to fall from the whisk or beater in a dissolving ribbon when it is lifted from the bowl. Beating constantly, pour in the warm milk in a slow, thin stream.

Then pour the egg-and-milk mixture back into the saucepan and, stirring constantly with a wooden spoon, cook over low heat until the custard thickens enough to coat the spoon like heavy cream. Do not let the custard come near a boil or it will curdle; if it gets too hot, lift the pan off the stove to cool it.

Strain the custard through a fine sieve into a large mixing bowl and set the bowl into a pot half filled with crushed ice or ice cubes and water. Stir the custard for 4 to 5 minutes, or until it is quite cold and begins to thicken. Beat thoroughly with a wire whisk to be sure it is perfectly smooth. Remove the bowl from the pot of ice and stir the reserved figs and the vanilla extract into the custard.

In a large bowl, beat the egg whites with a wire whisk or a rotary or electric beater until they are stiff enough to stand in unwavering peaks on the whisk or beater when it is lifted out of the bowl. In another bowl, but with the same beater, whip the cream until it is stiff and stands in firm peaks. With a rubber spatula, scoop the egg whites over the cream and fold them together gently but thoroughly. Pour in about one third of the custard-and-fig mixture and continue to fold until all the ingredients are well blended. Then fold in the rest of the custard-fig mixture.

With the spatula, scrape the entire contents of the bowl into a 3-quart decorative mold or two 9-by-5-by-3-inch loaf pans. Cover the mold or pans with foil and freeze the ice cream for 1 hour. With a table fork, scrape the frozen particles from the edges of the container and beat them into the ice cream. Freeze for 1 hour longer, scrape and beat the ice cream again, and return it to the freezer for at least 6 hours, or until it is firm.

To unmold and serve the fig ice cream, dip the mold or pan briefly into hot water. Place a chilled serving plate upside down over the mold and, grasping the plate and mold together firmly, invert them. Rap the plate on a table and the ice cream should slide out easily. Serve immediately or return to the freezer until ready to serve.

Pain Patate
YAM PUDDING

To serve 6 to 8

2 pounds yams	preferably freshly grated
1 tablespoon plus ½ pound butter, softened	½ teaspoon ground cinnamon
	1 teaspoon salt
2 cups unsifted flour	1½ cups sugar
1 teaspoon double-acting baking powder	4 eggs
	½ cup milk
1½ teaspoons ground nutmeg,	2 teaspoons vanilla extract

Translated literally, pain patate means "yam bread," but the dish is actually a kind of thick sweet pudding and is served as a dessert.

Drop the yams into enough boiling water to cover them by at least 1 inch and cook briskly, uncovered, until they show no resistance when pierced deeply with the point of a small sharp knife. Drain and peel the yams, then purée them through a potato ricer or food mill set over a bowl and set the purée aside.

Preheat the oven to 375°. With a pastry brush, spread 1 tablespoon of the softened butter evenly over the bottom and sides of a 13-by-9-by-2-inch baking dish. Combine the flour, baking powder, nutmeg, cinnamon and salt, sift them into a bowl and set aside.

In a deep bowl, cream the remaining ½ pound of softened butter and the sugar together by beating and mashing them against the sides of the bowl with the back of a large spoon until the mixture is light and fluffy. Beat in the eggs, one at a time. Add about 1 cup of the flour mixture and, when it is well incorporated, beat in about ¼ cup of the milk. Repeat, alternating 1 cup of the flour mixture with ¼ cup of milk and beating well after each addition. Stir in the puréed yams and the vanilla extract.

Pour the batter into the prepared baking dish, spreading it evenly and smoothing the top with a rubber spatula. Bake in the middle of the oven for 45 minutes, or until the top is golden brown and firm to the touch. Serve the *pain patate* at once, directly from the baking dish.

Croquignoles
DEEP-FRIED PASTRIES

To make about 3 dozen round or
    triangular pastries

2 cups unsifted flour
1 teaspoon double-acting baking
    powder
½ teaspoon ground nutmeg,
    preferably freshly grated
½ teaspoon salt

3 eggs
½ cup sugar
1 tablespoon butter, melted and
    cooled
1 tablespoon vanilla extract
Vegetable oil for deep frying
Confectioners' sugar

Combine the flour, baking powder, nutmeg and salt, sift them together into a bowl, and set aside.

In a deep mixing bowl, beat the eggs with a wire whisk until they are light and frothy. With a wooden spoon, beat in the sugar, the cooled melted butter and the vanilla extract and, when all the ingredients are thoroughly incorporated, beat in the flour mixture, about ½ cup at a time. Divide the dough into two equal portions.

To shape the dough into rounds, roll out one portion into a rough rectangle about ⅛ inch thick. With a cookie cutter or the rim of a glass, cut the dough into 3-inch rounds. Gather the scraps into a ball, roll them out as before and cut as many more rounds as you can. With a sharp knife, cut two parallel slashes about 2 inches long and ½ inch apart in the center of each round.

To shape the dough into triangles, roll out one portion into a circle about 12 inches in diameter and ⅛ inch thick. With a pastry wheel or sharp knife, divide the circle into 16 equal pie-shaped wedges. Cut a 3-inch slash lengthwise down the center of each wedge.

Pour vegetable oil into a deep fryer or large heavy saucepan to a depth of 2 or 3 inches and heat the oil until it reaches a temperature of 360° on a deep-frying thermometer.

Fry the *croquignoles,* two or three at a time, turning them about with a slotted spoon for 4 minutes, or until they are golden brown and crisp. As they are deep-fried, transfer them to paper towels to drain.

Serve the *croquignoles* warm, or cooled to room temperature. Just before serving, sprinkle them lightly with confectioners' sugar.

Oreilles de Cochon

DEEP-FRIED PASTRIES SHAPED LIKE PIG'S EARS

To make 16 eight-inch round
    pastries

2 cups unsifted flour
2 teaspoons double-acting baking
    powder
½ teaspoon salt
2 eggs
8 tablespoons butter, melted and
    cooled

Vegetable oil for deep frying
2 cups pure cane syrup *(see
    Glossary, page 150),* or substitute
    1⅓ cups dark corn syrup mixed
    with ⅔ cup dark molasses
1 cup coarsely chopped pecans

Combine the flour, baking powder and salt, sift them together into a bowl and set aside. In a deep bowl, beat the eggs to a froth with a wire whisk or a fork. Beating constantly, gradually pour in the cooled melted butter. Then stir in the flour mixture ½ cup at a time. Divide the dough into 16 equal portions and shape each portion into a 1-inch ball. On a lightly floured surface, roll each ball into a paper-thin round about 8 inches in diameter.

Pour vegetable oil to a depth of about 1½ inches into a heavy skillet or casserole at least 10 inches in diameter and 2 inches deep. Heat the oil to a temperature of 350° on a deep-frying thermometer.

To make each pastry, slide a round of dough into the skillet. As soon as the round rises to the surface of the oil, pierce its center with the tines of a long-handled fork. Rotate the fork clockwise, flattening the tines against the dough, to simultaneously twist the center of the round and fold the far side over on itself. Turn the pastry and brown it for a minute. Then transfer it to paper towels to drain while you fry the rest.

While the pastries are still hot, combine the cane syrup and pecans in a small saucepan and stir over low heat until the syrup is warm and fluid. Then dribble about 2 tablespoons of the cane-syrup mixture over the top of each pastry. Serve the *oreilles de cochon* warm or at room temperature.

Petits Fours

To make 5 dozen 1½-inch-square
    cakes

CAKE

2 tablespoons butter, softened, plus
    6 tablespoons butter, cut into ½-
    inch bits
2 tablespoons unsifted flour plus
    ½ cup flour, sifted before
    measuring
½ cup cornstarch, sifted before
    measuring
6 eggs, at room temperature
1 cup granulated sugar
1 teaspoon vanilla extract

Preheat the oven to 350°. With a pastry brush, spread 1 tablespoon of the softened butter over the bottom and sides of a 17-by-11-by-1-inch jelly-roll pan. Cut a piece of wax paper 19 to 20 inches long and fit it lengthwise into the pan, pressing it firmly into the bottom and against the ends. Brush the wax paper with the remaining tablespoon of softened butter, then sprinkle in the 2 tablespoons of unsifted flour and tip the pan to distribute it evenly. Invert the pan and rap the bottom sharply to remove the excess flour. Combine the ½ cup of sifted flour and the cornstarch, sift them together into a bowl and set aside.

In a small heavy saucepan, melt the 6 tablespoons of butter bits over low heat, stirring so that they melt completely without browning. Remove the pan from the heat, then skim off and discard the foam. Tipping the pan slightly, spoon the clear butter into a bowl and reserve it. Discard the milky solids that settle in the bottom of the pan.

Set a large heatproof mixing bowl over a pan of hot water off the heat. Place the eggs and the cup of granulated sugar in the bowl and, with a wire whisk or a rotary or electric beater, beat until they are thick, foamy and lukewarm. The sugar should be dissolved. Remove the bowl from the pan and continue to beat until the egg mixture has almost tripled in volume. It should be thick enough to stand in peaks when the beater is lifted from the bowl. (This will take about 15 minutes with an electric beater, and may require 30 minutes of continuous beating by hand.)

With a rubber spatula, gently fold in the flour-and-cornstarch mixture, a few tablespoonfuls at a time. Stir in the clarified butter, 1 teaspoon at a time, and add the vanilla extract.

Pour the batter into the paper-lined pan, spreading it evenly and smoothing the top with the spatula. Bake in the middle of the oven for 25 to 30 minutes, or until the cake begins to pull away from the sides of the pan and a toothpick or cake tester inserted in the center comes out clean. Remove the cake from the oven and carefully turn it out of the pan onto a fresh piece of wax paper. Gently peel off the layer of paper on top of the cake, then set the cake aside to cool to room temperature.

RASPBERRY-KIRSCH FILLING
¾ cup raspberry preserves
3 tablespoons kirsch

Meanwhile, prepare the fillings. For the raspberry-kirsch filling, melt the preserves in a small pan set over low heat, and pour them through a sieve into a bowl to strain out the seeds. Cool, then stir in the kirsch.

COFFEE FILLING
¼ cup coffee liqueur
1 tablespoon granulated sugar

1 tablespoon water
2 teaspoons instant coffee,
   preferably instant *espresso*

For the coffee filling, combine the coffee liqueur, 1 tablespoon of granulated sugar, 1 tablespoon water and 2 teaspoons of instant coffee in a small bowl and stir until the ingredients are well mixed.

CHOCOLATE AND MINT-CHOCOLATE
   FILLINGS
12 ounces semisweet chocolate,
   coarsely chopped
16 tablespoons butter (2 quarter-

pound sticks), cut into ½-inch
bits
2 cups confectioners' sugar
2 to 3 tablespoons crème de menthe

For the chocolate and mint-chocolate fillings, combine the 12 ounces of semisweet chocolate and 16 tablespoons of butter bits in a heavy 2- to 3-quart saucepan and, stirring constantly, melt them together over low heat. Remove the pan from the heat and stir in the 2 cups of confectioners' sugar, about ½ cup at a time. Spoon half of the mixture into a small bowl and add 2 to 3 tablespoons of crème de menthe, according to taste.

When the cake is cool enough to handle, use a long knife with a sharp serrated blade to trim off the rough edges and make a 15-by-9-inch rectangle. Cut the cake crosswise and lengthwise into four 7½-by-4½-inch quarters. Brush any loose crumbs off the top.

Place one of the quarters on a flat surface and, holding it firmly in place with one hand, cut it horizontally in half to make two thin layers. Separate the layers, laying them cut side up, and brush one cut surface with the raspberry-kirsch filling. Reassemble the cake with the filling in the center and cover it tightly with foil or plastic wrap. Repeat the entire procedure with the three remaining cake quarters, spreading them successively with the coffee, chocolate and mint-chocolate fillings. To facilitate the final cutting of the cakes, freeze them for about 1 hour.

Continued on next page   137

ICING

5 cups granulated sugar	sugar, sifted
2½ cups water	Red and green liquid food coloring
1½ cups light corn syrup	2 teaspoons instant coffee,
12 cups (4 pounds) confectioners'	preferably instant *espresso*

When you are ready to cut and ice the petits fours, prepare the icing in the following fashion: Combine the 5 cups of granulated sugar, the 2½ cups of water and the corn syrup in a heavy 6- to 8-quart casserole and stir over low heat until the sugar is dissolved. Using a hair-bristled (not nylon) pastry brush that has been dipped in cold water, wipe the sugar crystals that have formed on the sides of the pan back down into the syrup. Cover the pan tightly and cook the syrup over low heat for 5 minutes; its steam will dissolve any remaining crystals.

Increase the heat to high and boil the syrup uncovered and undisturbed for 5 minutes. Then remove the casserole from the heat and let the syrup cool to room temperature. (There will be about 4 cups of syrup.) Stirring the mixture constantly with a wire whisk, add the 12 cups of confectioners' sugar about 1 cupful at a time and beat until the ingredients are well combined. Place the casserole over low heat and, still stirring constantly, cook the icing until it is lukewarm and appears smooth and shiny. Do not let the icing overheat or it will lose its gloss.

Ladle or pour the icing into four small heavy saucepans (preferably pans with pouring spouts), dividing it equally among them. For the raspberry-kirsch-filled cakes, stir a few drops of red food coloring into one pan of icing to tint it pink. For the coffee-filled cakes, add 2 teaspoons of instant coffee to another pan and stir until the coffee dissolves and the icing is light brown. For the mint-chocolate-filled cakes, mix a few drops of green food coloring into another pan of icing to tint it green. For the chocolate-filled cakes, leave the fourth pan of icing white.

Each quarter of the cake is cut into petits fours and iced separately. Remove one quarter from the freezer, check its filling, and select the appropriate icing. Let the other three pans of icing cool to room temperature, then cover them tightly with plastic wrap until you are ready to use them. Just before using each one, warm it over low heat.

With a large sharp knife, cut the quarter cake into 15 individual cakes, each 1½ inches square. Arrange the cakes an inch or so apart on wire racks set in a large shallow baking pan. Pour the icing generously over the tops of the cakes, letting it spread by itself and run down the sides.

With a metal spatula, scrape the excess icing from the bottom of the baking pan and return it to the saucepan. Stirring constantly, warm the icing over low heat until it is fluid again. Then pour it over any of the cakes that were not evenly coated before.

CAKE DECORATIONS (OPTIONAL)

15 crystallized violets	8 tablespoons butter, softened
1½ ounces semisweet chocolate,	2 cups confectioners' sugar
coarsely chopped	Red and green liquid food coloring

If you like you can decorate the petits fours as shown on page 89. To ornament each white cake, center a crystallized violet in the top, pressing it gently into the icing. To trim the light brown cakes, melt 1½ ounces of coarsely chopped semisweet chocolate in a small heavy pan set over low heat and, using a fork, dribble lines of chocolate onto the tops of the cakes. For a more precise pattern, roll a piece of wax paper into a cone, cut off the bottom point to make a small hole and squeeze the chocolate through it onto the cakes.

To ornament the pink and green petits fours, cream the 8 tablespoons of softened butter by beating and mashing it against the sides of a bowl with the back of a large spoon until it is light and fluffy. Beat in the 2 cups of confectioners' sugar, about ½ cup at a time, and stir to a smooth, thick paste. Spoon half the mixture into another bowl and stir in two drops of red food coloring to shade it a dark pink. Add two drops of green food coloring to the paste remaining in the first bowl and stir until it is dark green. Using a pastry bag fitted with the decorative tips of your choice, pipe the pink paste onto the pink petits fours in whatever design you like, and pipe ribbons of the green paste onto the green petits fours.

Leave the petits fours uncovered for about 1 hour to let the icing dry completely. Then drape them loosely with wax paper. They can safely be kept at room temperature for about 24 hours.

You can repeat the entire procedure—scraping, warming, and pouring the icing—as many times as necessary but be careful never to let the icing become too hot or it will lose its gloss.

Let the iced cakes dry on the racks for about 10 minutes, then transfer them to plates or wax paper. Following the same techniques identically, cut the three remaining cake quarters one at a time and cover the petits fours with the appropriate icing.

Bâtons de Noisettes
NUT STICKS

To make about thirty 2½-inch-
long sticks

1 tablespoon plus ½ pound
  unsalted butter, softened
¼ cup granulated sugar
¼ teaspoon salt

2 cups unsifted flour
2 teaspoons vanilla extract
1 cup finely chopped walnuts or
  filberts
1 cup confectioners' sugar

Preheat the oven to 350°. With a pastry brush, spread the tablespoon of softened butter evenly over a large baking sheet and set it aside.

In a deep bowl, cream the remaining ½ pound of the softened butter with the granulated sugar by beating and mashing them against the sides of the bowl with the back of a large spoon until light and fluffy. Sprinkle the salt over the flour and add the flour mixture to the butter ½ cup at a time, beating after each addition. Beat in the vanilla and chopped nuts.

To shape each *bâton,* cut off a heaping tablespoon of the dough and roll it with your hands into a cylinder about 2½ inches long and ½ inch in diameter. Arrange the *bâtons* 1 inch apart on the buttered baking sheet and bake them in the middle of the oven for 10 to 12 minutes, or until they are a delicate golden color.

With a wide metal spatula, transfer the *bâtons* to wire racks. When they are completely cool, roll each cookie in the confectioners' sugar to coat it evenly on all sides. In a tightly covered jar or tin, *bâtons de noisettes* can safely be kept for several weeks.

Creole Macaroons

To make about 40 three-inch round
  cookies

2 tablespoons butter, softened
4 egg yolks
2 cups sugar
¼ cup finely grated fresh orange
  peel

1 cup (4 ounces) finely ground
  blanched almonds
1 cup whole-wheat flour
4 egg whites
2½ cups (12 ounces) slivered
  blanched almonds

Preheat the oven to 350°. With a pastry brush, spread the softened butter evenly over two large baking sheets. Set the sheets aside.

In a deep bowl, stir the egg yolks and sugar together with a wooden spoon. When they are well mixed, beat in the orange peel and add the ground almonds and the whole-wheat flour, about ½ cup at a time. Continue to stir to make a smooth, thick pastelike dough.

With a wire whisk or a rotary or electric beater, beat the egg whites until they are stiff enough to stand in unwavering peaks on the whisk or beater when it is lifted out of the bowl. Using a rubber spatula, fold in the slivered almonds, then scoop the egg-white mixture over the dough and fold the dough and mixture together gently but thoroughly.

To shape each macaroon, brush your hands with flour, break off a tablespoonful of the dough and gently roll it between your palms into a ball about 1½ inches in diameter. Arrange the balls 2 inches apart on the buttered baking sheets to allow them to spread into 3-inch rounds.

Bake the macaroons in the middle of the oven for 10 to 12 minutes, or until the edges are delicately browned. With a large metal spatula, transfer the cookies to wire racks to cool before serving. In a tightly covered jar or tin, Creole macaroons can safely be kept for about a week.

Pecan Lace Cookies

To make about 30 four-inch round cookies

6 tablespoons butter, softened
4 tablespoons plus ½ cup unsifted flour
1 teaspoon double-acting baking powder
A pinch of salt
2 cups sugar
2 eggs, well beaten
1 teaspoon vanilla extract
2 cups coarsely chopped pecans

Preheat the oven to 400°. With a pastry brush, spread 2 tablespoons of the softened butter over two large baking sheets. Sprinkle each baking sheet with 1 tablespoon of the flour and tip the pan from side to side to distribute the flour evenly. Invert the baking sheet and rap it sharply to remove the excess flour. Combine ½ cup of the flour, the baking powder and the salt, and sift them together into a bowl. Set aside.

In a deep bowl, cream 2 tablespoons of softened butter by beating and mashing it against the sides of the bowl with the back of a spoon until it is light and fluffy. Add the sugar, beat in the eggs and the vanilla extract, and stir the flour mixture into the batter. Then add the pecans.

Drop the batter by the heaping teaspoonful onto the prepared baking sheets, spacing the cookies about 3 inches apart. Bake in the middle of the oven for 5 minutes, or until the cookies have spread into lacelike 4-inch rounds and have turned golden brown. Let the cookies cool for a minute or so, then transfer them to wire racks to cool completely.

Let the baking sheets cool completely, then coat them with the remaining 2 tablespoons of softened butter and 2 tablespoons of flour, and bake the remaining cookies in the preheated oven. In a tightly covered jar or box, the cookies can safely be kept for a week or so.

Almond Nougat

To make about eighty 1¼-inch
   squares

1½ cups coarsely chopped
   almonds (about ½ pound)
1 tablespoon butter, softened, plus
   2 tablespoons butter, cut into
   ½-inch bits
2½ cups granulated sugar

1¾ cups light corn syrup
3 egg whites
⅓ cup water
¾ cup confectioners' sugar
1 teaspoon vanilla extract
½ teaspoon salt

Preheat the oven to 350°. Spread the almonds in one layer in a shallow baking dish and, stirring occasionally, toast them in the middle of the oven for about 5 minutes, or until they are delicately browned. Remove the dish from the oven and set the almonds aside. With a pastry brush, spread the tablespoon of softened butter evenly over a large baking sheet. Set the baking sheet aside.

Combine ½ cup of the granulated sugar and 1 cup of the corn syrup in a heavy 2- to 3-quart saucepan and stir over moderate heat until the sugar dissolves. Raise the heat and boil briskly, uncovered and undisturbed, until the syrup reaches a temperature of 248° on a candy thermometer, or until a few drops spooned into ice water immediately forms a firm but still slightly pliable ball.

Watch the syrup carefully and when it begins to bubble and rise in the pan, reduce the heat for a few moments. When sugar crystals appear inside the pan, brush them back into the syrup with a natural-bristle (not nylon) pastry brush that has been lightly moistened with water.

Meanwhile, in the large bowl of a stationary electric beater, beat the egg whites at medium speed until they are stiff enough to stand in soft peaks on the beater when it is lifted out of the bowl.

Beating constantly at medium speed, pour in the syrup in a slow, thin stream and continue to beat for 4 to 5 minutes, or until the mixture is thick and begins to stiffen. Turn off the machine and let the candy mixture stand at room temperature while you prepare a second batch of syrup.

In a heavy 3- to 4-quart saucepan, combine the remaining 2 cups of granulated sugar, the remaining ¾ cup of corn syrup and the water, and stir over moderate heat until the sugar dissolves. Raise the heat and boil briskly, uncovered and undisturbed, until the syrup reaches a temperature of 272° on a candy thermometer, or until a drop spooned into ice water immediately separates into hard, but not brittle, threads. Watch the syrup carefully and adjust the heat when necessary.

Beating constantly at medium speed, pour the second batch of syrup into the egg-white-and-syrup mixture in a slow, thin stream. Continue to beat for about 10 minutes longer, or until the candy becomes opaque and creamy, then beat in the 2 tablespoons of butter bits and the confectioners' sugar, vanilla extract and salt. With a wooden spoon, stir in the reserved toasted almonds.

Working quickly, spread the nougat mixture in the buttered baking dish. Pat it to a thickness of about ¾ inch with the palms of your hands and smooth the top with a rolling pin. When the nougat cools to room temperature, cover it with wax paper and set it aside in a cool place (not the refrigerator) for at least 12 hours.

Cut the nougat into 1¼-inch squares and serve at once. Or packet each piece in a square of foil or plastic wrap and store the nougat in a tightly covered jar or tin until ready to serve.

Pecan Pralines

To make about 2 dozen 2½-inch
  round candies

⅓ cup light brown sugar
⅛ teaspoon salt
1 teaspoon vanilla extract
2 cups (about ½ pound) coarsely
  chopped pecans

2 tablespoons butter, softened
¼ cup light cream or evaporated
  milk
2 cups granulated sugar
½ cup water

With a pastry brush, spread the softened butter on the bottom of two large baking sheets or jelly-roll pans. Set them aside.

Warm the light cream or evaporated milk over low heat in a small saucepan. When bubbles begin to form around the edges of the pan, remove the pan from the heat and cover it tightly to keep the cream or evaporated milk warm.

Combine the granulated sugar and water in a 10-inch cast-iron or enameled-iron skillet about 2 inches deep and bring to a boil over high heat, stirring until the sugar dissolves. Reduce the heat to moderate and, gripping a pot holder in each hand, tip the pan back and forth gently until the syrup turns a rich, golden brown. This may take 10 minutes or more.

As soon as the syrup reaches the correct color, remove the skillet from the heat and, with a wooden spoon, stir in the brown sugar and salt. Stirring constantly, pour in the warm cream or evaporated milk in a slow, thin stream. Add the vanilla extract, and then stir in the pecans.

To form each praline, ladle about 4 teaspoons of the pecan mixture onto a buttered baking sheet. As you proceed, space the pralines about 3 inches apart to allow room for them to spread into 2½-inch rounds. When the pralines have cooled to room temperature, transfer them to a serving plate with a wide metal spatula.

NOTE: To make benne pralines, substitute ½ cup of sesame (or benne) seeds for the 2 cups of pecans. Before warming the cream or milk, place the seeds in a heavy ungreased 8-inch skillet and, stirring constantly, toast them over moderate heat for about 5 minutes, or until they are a delicate golden color. Then prepare the pralines as described above, adding the benne seeds after the vanilla extract is incorporated into the candy.

DRINKS

Creole Champagne Punch

To make about 5 quarts

1 large fresh ripe pineapple
1 pint firm fresh strawberries
1 pound superfine sugar
1 cup strained fresh lemon juice
1 cup strained fresh orange juice
½ cup curaçao or other orange-
flavored liqueur
1 quart champagne, chilled
1 quart dry white wine, chilled
1½ quarts (6 cups) club soda,
chilled

A 2- to 3-gallon punch bowl
A large solid block of ice

Place the pineapple on its side on a cutting board and, grasping it firmly with one hand, slice off the leafy crown and the base with a large sharp knife. Stand the pineapple on end and slice off the prickly rind in seven or eight downward strokes, cutting deep enough each time to remove the eyes. Then divide the fruit lengthwise into quarters and cut the triangular section of core away from each quarter. Cut two of the quarters lengthwise in half and slice each of these crosswise into ½-inch-thick wedges. Grate the remaining two quarters of the pineapple on the teardrop-shaped holes of a stand-up hand grater. Set aside the pineapple wedges and grated pineapple.

Pick over the strawberries carefully, removing the stems and hulls and discarding any fruit that is badly bruised or shows signs of mold. Wash briefly in a sieve or colander set under cold running water, then spread the berries on paper towels to drain and pat them completely dry with fresh paper towels.

Just before serving, combine the superfine sugar, lemon and orange juice, and curaçao in the punch bowl and stir to dissolve the sugar completely. Stir in the champagne, wine and club soda. Carefully place the solid block of ice in the bowl, then stir the pineapple wedges, grated pineapple and strawberries into the punch.

Milk Punch

To make 1 serving

⅓ cup light cream
2 ounces bourbon
2 teaspoons confectioners' sugar
⅛ teaspoon vanilla extract
3 or 4 ice cubes

Ground nutmeg, preferably freshly grated

An 8-ounce double old-fashioned glass, chilled

Combine the cream, bourbon, sugar, vanilla extract and ice cubes in a mixing glass and place a bar shaker on top. Firmly grasp the glass and shaker together with both hands and shake vigorously 9 or 10 times. Remove the shaker, place a strainer over the mixing glass and pour the milk punch into the chilled old-fashioned glass. Sprinkle the top lightly with nutmeg and serve at once.

Gin Fizz

To make 1 tall drink

2 egg whites
4 teaspoons superfine sugar
½ cup light cream
2 ounces gin
4 teaspoons strained fresh lemon juice

½ teaspoon orange-flower water
¼ teaspoon vanilla extract
3 to 4 ice cubes

A 10-ounce Tom Collins glass, chilled

The gin fizz was invented in 1888 by Henry C. Ramos of the Imperial Cabaret in New Orleans. The formula for the original Ramos gin fizz has never been disclosed, but the following recipe is a favorite version of the drink today.

Combine the egg whites and sugar in a mixing glass and stir with a bar spoon until the sugar dissolves. Add the cream, gin, lemon juice, orange-flower water, vanilla extract and ice cubes.

Place a bar shaker on top of the mixing glass and, grasping the glass and shaker firmly together with both hands, shake vigorously 9 or 10 times. Remove the shaker, place a strainer over the mixing glass and pour the gin fizz into the chilled Tom Collins glass.

Absinthe

The people of Louisiana have long had a passion for mixed drinks; in fact, the very word cocktail is said to be a corruption of the word *coquetier,* or egg cup—the type of vessel that a New Orleans apothecary, A. A. Peychaud, used for serving mixed drinks nearly two centuries ago. Among the potables favored as a mixer in decades past was absinthe—a highly alcoholic (136 proof) green liqueur flavored with wormwood, anise and other aromatic herbs. The drink takes its name from the botanical term for wormwood, *Artemisia absinthium,* a plant whose medicinal properties had been highly prized since the days of the ancient Greeks; absinthe itself was originally a stomach tonic, concocted in Switzerland by a French physician, Dr. Pierre Ordinaire, who had fled to that country during the French Revolution. In 1797 Dr. Ordinaire's heirs sold the recipe for absinthe to Henri-Louis Pernod, who later bottled the drink commercially under the Pernod name. Its potency, flavor and reputation as a tonic (and aphrodisiac) made it popular in both Europe and Louisiana during the 19th Century. At one point, New Orleans was called the absinthe capital of the world.

Too strong and bitter to be drunk straight, absinthe was customarily diluted with water. The correct ritual called for pouring the absinthe into a glass filled with ice, setting a specially designed perforated spoon on top of the glass and placing a cube of sugar in the spoon. Water was then poured slowly over the sugar and dripped through it to make the absinthe clouded or milky.

By the early 20th Century it became clear that absinthe was dangerous. One of its ingredients, wormwood, proved habit-forming and the cause of convulsions, delirium, hallucinations, permanent mental derangement and even death. The sale of absinthe was banned in Switzerland in 1908, in the United States in 1912 and in France in 1915. The liqueur is nearly extinct today and its sale prohibited in most countries.

When absinthe vanished from Louisiana, other anise-flavored drinks took its place. Among the local favorites are Ojen, imported from Spain, and an American-made liqueur called Herbsaint, first bottled commercially by a New Orleans apothecary named J. Marion Legendre in 1934. The Pernod company, which long since stopped making absinthe, now produces instead a sweet, anise-flavored liqueur that contains no wormwood.

Though asbinthe itself is gone, its name lingers on in such drinks as the absinthe *suissesse* and absinthe frappé, for which recipes are given here and on the following pages.

Absinthe Frappé

To make 1 cocktail

2 ounces Herbsaint or Pernod
½ teaspoon superfine sugar

1 cup shaved or finely cracked ice

A 6-ounce champagne glass, chilled

Combine the Herbsaint or Pernod and sugar in a mixing glass and stir with a bar spoon to dissolve the sugar. Fill the champagne glass with the ice, pour the Herbsaint or Pernod mixture over the ice and serve at once.

Absinthe Suissesse

To make 1 cocktail

1½ ounces Herbsaint, Pernod or
   Ojen
2 tablespoons light cream
1 egg white
1 tablespoon orgeat syrup *(see*

Glossary, page 150)
½ cup shaved or finely cracked ice

An 8-ounce wine or old-fashioned
   glass, chilled
A short straw

Combine the Herbsaint, Pernod or Ojen, cream, egg white, orgeat syrup and ice in the jar of an electric blender and blend at high speed for 5 seconds. Pour the absinthe *suissesse,* unstrained, into the chilled glass and serve at once with a short straw.

Ojen Cocktail

To make 1 cocktail

1½ ounces Ojen
3 dashes Peychaud bitters *(see*
   Glossary, page 150)

3 or 4 ice cubes

A 3-ounce wine or cocktail glass,
   chilled

Ojen (pronounced oh-hen) is an anise-flavored apéritif popular in Louisiana. Its name comes from the Spanish word for wormwood, ajenjo, because Ojen tastes somewhat like absinthe.

Combine the Ojen, Peychaud bitters and ice cubes in a mixing glass and place a bar shaker on top. Firmly grasp the glass and shaker together with both hands and shake vigorously 9 or 10 times. Remove the shaker, place a strainer over the mixing glass and pour the Ojen cocktail into the chilled wine or cocktail glass. Serve at once.

Sazerac

To make 1 cocktail

2½ ounces bourbon or rye
4 teaspoons superfine sugar
½ teaspoon Peychaud bitters
   (see Glossary, page 150)
¼ teaspoon Angostura bitters

3 or 4 ice cubes
3 dashes Herbsaint or Pernod
A twist of fresh lemon peel

A 4-ounce old-fashioned glass,
   chilled

This cocktail is named for Sazerac-de-Forge brandy, with which it was originally made in the Sazerac Coffee House in New Orleans in antebellum days. After the Civil War, tastes in liquor changed and the brandy was replaced by whiskey. About 1870 an inspired bartender began the custom of rinsing the glass with absinthe before pouring in the whiskey mixture. Since 1912, when the sale of absinthe was made illegal, Pernod or Herbsaint has been used instead.

Combine the bourbon or rye, sugar, Peychaud bitters, Angostura bitters and ice cubes in a mixing glass and stir with a bar spoon to dissolve the sugar. Pour the Herbsaint or Pernod into the chilled old-fashioned glass and tip the glass from side to side to coat it evenly; then pour out and discard the liqueur. Place a strainer over the mixing glass, pour the Sazerac into the old-fashioned glass, drop in the lemon twist and serve at once. (Though it is not traditional, you may add ice cubes to the cocktail and serve it on the rocks.)

Café Brûlot

To serve 6

The peel of 1 orange, cut into
   1-by-⅛-inch strips
The peel of 1 lemon, cut into
   1-by-⅛-inch strips
3 sugar lumps
6 whole cloves

A 2-inch cinnamon stick
1 cup cognac
½ cup curaçao or other orange
   liqueur
2 cups fresh strong black coffee,
   preferably made from dark roast
   Creole-style ground coffee

Assemble the ingredients for the *café brûlot* at the dinner table and prepare it there in the following manner: Light the burner under a *brûlot* bowl or chafing-dish pan and adjust the heat to low. Drop the orange and lemon peel, sugar lumps, cloves and cinnamon stick into the bowl or pan, pour in the cognac and curaçao, and stir to dissolve the sugar. When the mixture is warm, ignite it with a match. Stirring gently, pour in the coffee in a slow, thin stream and continue to stir until the flames die. Ladle the *café brûlot* into *brûlot* or demitasse cups and serve at once.

HOW TO MAKE AUTHENTIC CREOLE COFFEE

Creole coffee is a unique brew and making it is something of a ritual. Though different cooks have personal variations, all recipes call for a dark roasted grind, usually flavored with chicory, and almost all insist on using a drip pot, like the one above. (This pot comes in 2-, 4- and 6-cup sizes; to order it by mail, see the Shopping Guide, page 150.) A Creole coffeepot consists of two containers: the top retains the grounds, and its perforated base permits the brew to drip down into the bottom container. For diffusing and dispersing the brew more evenly there are two removable filters, one concave and the other convex, inside the top part of the pot. To make four coffee cups or eight demitasse cups of Creole coffee, bring three 8-ounce measuring cups of water to a boil in a kettle. Meanwhile, assemble the pot and set the convex filter in place. Measure 6 tablespoons of ground coffee over this filter and put the concave filter into the top of the pot as shown above. Pour about a tablespoonful of the boiling water into the top filter and let it flow through. Lift the top filter to check the grounds; when they stop bubbling, put the top filter back in place and pour in another tablespoon or so of boiling water. Repeat the procedure until all 3 cups of water have dripped through. Since the procedure may take as long as 20 minutes, you may keep the coffee hot by setting the pot in a saucepan partly filled with boiling water. Serve the coffee as soon as it is brewed or keep it hot by changing the water in the saucepan. Never set the drip pot directly on the stove to heat the coffee.

Glossary

Absinthe: Bitter anise-flavored green liqueur. Because it contains the dangerous oils of wormwood, the sale of true absinthe is prohibited in most countries.

Beans, small red: Flat oval-shaped dried beans, smaller than red kidney beans and darker in color than pinto beans. Red kidney beans can be substituted.

Cane syrup, pure (ribbon cane syrup): Sweet dark-brown sugar-cane syrup, with a flavor somewhat like that of dark-brown sugar. Available in 12-, 24-, 45- and 90-fluid-ounce cans. As a substitute, combine two parts dark corn syrup with one part dark molasses.

Corn flour: Yellow or white corn, milled to the texture of wheat flour. It tastes like cornmeal.

Crawfish (crayfish): Fresh-water crustacean, highly valued for the sweet white meat.

Creole mustard: Pungent prepared mustard made from brown mustard seeds. As a substitute, use any strong-flavored prepared brown mustard.

Filé powder: Ground dried sassafras leaves for flavoring and thickening gumbo.

Herbsaint: Greenish-amber anise-flavored liqueur.

Jerusalem artichoke: Edible tuber of a variety of sunflower native to the United States. The tubers look like small rough-skinned sweet potatoes, but their flesh is white.

Mirliton (vegetable pear, chayote, *christophene*): Tropical squash, available in the Louisiana area in early fall, and in some Latin American markets elsewhere the year round.

Ojen: Anise-flavored 84-proof liqueur made in Spain.

Orange-flower water: A subtle flavoring made from orange blossoms steeped in water.

Orgeat: A syrup prepared from powdered dried almonds.

Pernod: Anise-flavored apéritif, made in France.

Peychaud bitters: Spicy red flavoring introduced to New Orleans in the 1790s by A. A. Peychaud, an apothecary. Other kinds of bitters may be substituted for Peychaud.

Ponce: In Louisiana, a pig's stomach is filled with a spicy meat-and-yam mixture and steamed to produce an oversized sausage called a stuffed *ponce.*

Redfish (red drum, channel bass): Copper- or bronze-colored salt-water inshore commercial or game fish with a distinctive black spot at the base of the tail.

Rice, broken: A name sometimes used for short-grain rice, which produces a stickier jambalaya than the long-grain variety.

River shrimp: Tiny fresh-water shrimp found in the Mississippi and other Louisiana rivers and available only in that area.

Roux: A mixture of flour and fat used as a thickening agent for sauces, soups and gravies.

Sauterne: A white domestic table wine, not the French Sauternes.

Trout, speckled: Louisiana name for the spotted sea trout. It is related to the weakfish or gray sea trout, which may be used as a substitute.

Yam: In most Southern states, the preferred sweet potato is the orange-fleshed moist variety commonly called a yam.

Shopping Guide

Most of the ingredients and utensils called for in this book's recipes can be found at any grocery or supermarket, or in a housewares shop. Even such distinctively Creole and Acadian products as crawfish and filé powder are sometimes available at fine food stores. For information about sources f Herbsaint or Peychaud bitters your area, you may write to Sa erac Co., Inc., 328 N. Cortez S P.O. Box 52821, New Orleans, l 70150. The following places a cept mail orders for the produ specified, but—because polic differ and managements char —it is best to write to them l fore ordering to determine wl they have in stock:

Pure ribbon cane syrup and La Cuite
C. S. Steen Syrup Mill, Inc.
P.O. Box 339
Abbeville, La. 70510

Smoked sausage
Bourgeois Meat Market
519 Schriever Highway
Thibodaux, La. 70301

Creole cream cheese
Borden, Inc.
P.O. Box 10098
New Orleans, La. 70121

Live crawfish, frozen crawfish meat, redfish and speckled trout
Battistella's Sea Foods, Inc.
910 Touro St.
New Orleans, La. 70116

Food-coloring paste
Wilton Enterprises, Inc.
833 West 115 St.
Chicago, Ill. 60643

Creole drip coffeepots, cast-iro cooking pots
La Nasa Hardware Co., Inc.
1027 Decatur St.
New Orleans, La. 70116

Peychaud bitters, dark roast an chicory coffee, filé powder, Cre mustard, orange-flower water, orgeat syrup, pecans
Gourmet Shop
D. H. Holmes Co., Ltd.
819 Canal St.
New Orleans, La. 70112

Dried red beans, corn flour, da roast and chicory coffee, filé powder, Creole mustard, short grain rice, smoked sausages, Steen's pure ribbon cane syrup and La Cuite
Frank A. Von der Haar
4238 Magazine St.
New Orleans, La. 70115

Recipe Index

NOTE: Size, weight and material are specified for pans in the recipes because they affect cooking results. A pan should be just large enough to hold its contents comfortably. Heavy pans heat slowly and cook food at a constant rate. Aluminum and cast iron conduct heat well but may discolor foods that are made with egg yolks, wine, vinegar or lemon. Enamelware is a fairly poor conductor of heat. Many recipes recommend stainless steel or enameled cast iron, which do not have these faults.

Poultry and Meats

Vegetables, Pickles and Preserves

Breads

Desserts and Candies

Drinks

Photographs on pages 45 and 63 by Richard Jeffery. Illustration on page 17 by Albert Sherman; illustration on page 149 by Robert Geissman.